Reviews for
Embezzlement: How to Detect, Prevent and .

CW01337516

"A thoroughly enjoyable and accessible read — chock full of stories that bring the subject of pink-collar crime to life. Kelly Paxton helps us understand that fraud happens in all aspects of our personal and professional lives. She opens our eyes to the realities of fraud and gives thoughtful tips to deal with it. A must read for everyone — whether you have seen or experienced fraud first-hand or not."

> — **BETHMARA KESSLER-SPEAKER**, Chair, ACFE Board of Regents

"Kelly has done an amazing job of capturing the essence of employee fraud schemes on businesses, warnings of active fraud, and preventing these devastating incidents to organizations. She explains it all with her hands-on investigation results and actual fraud stories pulled from the headlines. This book is a must-read for all business leaders and owners who want to be aware of fraud in their organization and reduce the likelihood of fraud occurring on their watch. Yes, it can happen in your organization!"

> — **DAN RAMEY**, CPA, CFE, CFF — President, Houston Financial Forensics, LLC

"Kelly Paxton's book is concise, informative, and applicable to a variety of readers. The numerous real-life examples of pink-collar crime emphasize her point that the crimes are prevalent and anyone can be a victim. Her prevention techniques should be used by organizations of all types and sizes as checklists for crime prevention, crime reporting, and recovery after victimization."

> — **EMILY M. HOMER, PHD**, Assistant Professor of Criminology and Criminal Justice

"Fraud comes in many forms—from simple theft by swiping a few dollars from your mom's wallet to technically sophisticated, movie-ready *Casino Royale*-like scripts. The word "fraud" is so generic that one can find myriad applications, making seemingly everyone an expert in such a loosely defined field. In the past twenty years, I've seen FBI agents turned celebrity thanks to movies like *Wolf on Wall Street* alongside famed convicted hacker hoodlums, each professing to know and teach about fraud. Their backgrounds and experiences make them interesting, perhaps even sexy (if fraud could ever be considered sexy), but it doesn't make them well-rounded like Kelly Paxton. Paxton's dedication and earnest work on pink-collar crime dates back a decade. Her focus, experience, and resilience in professing, sharing, and training in this unique and often overlooked criminal activity stands alone. *Embezzlement* exemplifies real experiences, tactics, and investigative solutions for this least-suspecting yet growing criminal element representing nearly half of the total labor force: Women. Fraud examiners, investigators, and industry pros will be grabbing *Embezzlement* off the shelf and find it hard to put down."

  — **CYNTHIA HETHERINGTON**, President, Hetherington Group

"Kelly Paxton is one of the best financial fraud investigators of our time, uncovering crimes of fraud and embezzlement with an acumen for taking complex evidence, and relaying it in a way that tells a compelling story. Kelly's trainings on these topics demonstrate not only her expertise in this field, but also give the audience an entertaining and informative experience that leaves them on the edge of their seat."

  — **CHRISTINA FISCELLA**, Professional Fraud Investigator, Public Speaker

"What a fantastic book by fraud-fighter Kelly Paxton! It's an easy read that combines interesting embezzlement stories, relevant fraud concepts, and excellent fraud prevention tips. Kelly's discussion of what constitutes pink-collar crime was enlightening. This is a must read for any conscientious business owner looking for practical advice on reducing their exposure to employee fraud."

  — **TRACY COENEN**, Forensic Accountant

"Kelly Paxton uses her passion for the psychology of money to raise fraud awareness. Her experience and humor help the reader understand pink-collar crime and its devastating effects. Her book is a fascinating read. It provides several practical ways for people to protect themselves and ways to help identify pink flags."

— **ROBYN SHAW, CPA, CFE**, Owner of Facts & Figures Forensics

"You will not regret picking up this witty, honest, and eye-opening book on embezzlement. Kelly shares her very own real-life stories as well as the best ones in the news in the perfect way. Kelly's work and guidance on pink-collar crime cannot be matched anywhere. Her prevention tips are perfect for individuals as well as organizations of any type or size."

— **AMANDA JO ERVEN**, Audit and Ethics Consultant & Speaker

"In this book, Kelly covers it all — tips for fraud prevention and early detection, lots of examples that illustrate the different sides of the fraud triangle, and action items for dealing with fraud after the fact. A must-read for anyone who needs to understand the fraudster's motivation behind this unique crime and how to fight it."

— **MARCY PHELPS**, CFE, Marcy Phelps & Associates Inc.

"The name Kelly Paxton has become synonymous with pink-collar crime and no one knows it any better. Kelly channels her years of personal experience into real-life examples and prevention methods that give you some practical skills, know-how and prevention tips in a fun, light-hearted way. This is a great addition to your fraud library."

— **BRIAN WILLINGHAM**, CFE, Diligentia

"Kelly has brought into the light one of the more interesting aspects of the fraud perpetrator: many are women. With this, the era of 'I never suspected, her…,' 'Who would believe that she…?' and the classic 'It's never who you think!' will be coming to a close."

— **ALLAN BACHMAN**, CFE, ACFE Education Manager (retired)

"An eye opening and thought-provoking must read for every small business owner and department manager. Kelly illustrates very clearly how occupation fraud can, and does, happen frequently in environments built on trust. Well written, engaging embezzlement stories keep you entertained, and straight forward simple prevention steps are clearly laid out to prevent it from happening to you."

— **MARY BRESLIN,** CFE, CIA

"Kelly's book on embezzlement and pink-collar crime is an absolute treasure. It is timely, well-researched and cleverly written. She's added plenty of unbelievable examples of real-life cases. It is a must-have for investigators, accountants and business owners."

— **SCOTT FULMER**, Utah Private Investigator, Author of *Confessions of a Private Eye*

"Written by one of the most well-respected fraud investigators in the community, Kelly exposes the significance and materiality of pink-collar criminals written in a way that both investigators and small business owners can learn how to better prevent fraud."

— **MATT CHRISTENSEN**, CFE

Embezzlement:
How to Prevent, Detect and
Investigate Pink-Collar Crime

By Kelly Paxton, CFE, PI

Library of Congress Cataloging-in-Publication Data
Names: Paxton, Kelly, author
Title: Crime prevention: approaches, practices and evaluations
Description: Self-published
Identifiers: ISBN
Subjects: Crime prevention—United States
ISBN: 9798578059711
Author's website: https://pinkcollarcrime.com and kellypaxton.com
Twitter: #pinkcollarcrime
Facebook: @pinkcollarcrime
LinkedIn: https://www.linkedin.com/in/kellypaxton

Dedication

Richard, you have always been there. I couldn't ask for or want more.

Noah and Lili, stay being you. #proud

Table of Contents

Foreword

Shortly after earning my undergraduate degree in international studies and economics, I began a sensible career in finance. In hindsight, finance was not the best choice for me: money was. By "money," I mean analyzing how people make decisions regarding their assets—how they view, spend, earn, save and (sometimes) steal money over the course of their lives. I took a step in this direction with my second career in law enforcement, but it's my current job as an educator about fraud detection and prevention that best incorporates my passion for the psychology of money.

So how did I get here? Well, the abridged version is that I received a phone call while working at Piper Jaffray, a financial brokerage firm in Lake Oswego, Oregon. The special agent asked about a specific client whom I had always considered a bit suspicious, but this was the early '90s—we didn't have risk identification and compliance services like Know Your Customer® (KYC) in place. All I knew for certain was that the client, Allan, showed up one day with a big check in his pocket. He wanted to trade a lot, which made him a great client for the broker. "Churn and burn," they used to say. He didn't seem to care about the fees or risk. Later we found out why. The money was stolen. Allan had committed wire fraud and eventually he was arrested. A lesson I learned from that experience and subsequent years in the financial investigation field was that people don't care about taking care of money when they don't earn it through hard work.

A year after that, I left my job in finance to learn to shoot guns, drive fast cars and conduct surveillance at the Federal Law Enforcement Training Center in Brunswick, Georgia. I was now a special agent for the U.S. Customs Office of Investigations, now part of Homeland Security. I couldn't believe that I got paid to follow suspects, study bank statements, listen to phone calls and, when appropriate, make arrests. Most of the people I investigated were men, bad guys who dealt drugs, laundered money, preyed on children and committed fraud.

A markedly high point of my career was getting a female lawyer disbarred and sent to prison for stealing $2.4 million in an advance fee scheme. An advance fee scheme is a type of fraud that usually involves promising the victim a large share of a big amount of money in return for a "small" up-front payment, hence the "advance" term.

The lawyer was fueled by greed, much like the men who preceded her in committing crimes like this. But unlike them, it would have been easy for her to escape detection due to her respectable "good girl" image. I must say that my work was becoming increasingly interesting.

However, that was when my husband finished his Ph.D. and we moved to the Midwest. Despite the advantages of this new home, it didn't have a port of entry so my customs career came to a close. After three years staying at home with my kids, I was eager to rejoin the workforce. I dipped my toe in, hanging around the fringes of law enforcement by conducting background investigations for the federal government. Then, my family decided to move back home to Portland, Oregon where I accepted a position as an analyst on the Fraud Identity Theft Enforcement Team (FITE) at the local sheriff's office. While there I studied and obtained my Certified Fraud Examiner designation.

My job was to assist the detectives working on theft cases, generating what were called packages on the suspects, including spreadsheets, background information, etc. This work also included scheduling their banking information, meaning tracing funds in and out of suspects' bank accounts. As much as I liked all of my colleagues, Microsoft® Excel was definitely my best friend at the office. Smart, reliable and delightfully low-maintenance, good old Excel helped me see patterns in the data. For example, one standout pattern that came to light was that all but one of the suspects in my embezzlement cases were women. This simple observation led me down an exciting new path.

In studying the bank statements of suspects and victims alike, I noted that the excuses the suspects used were split. Some women stole to make ends meet, while others wanted to keep up with the Joneses, to "live the life." Regardless of their motives, what struck me was just how ordinary some of these female perpetrators were—from homemakers to long-term employees. These were not women that you, or anyone else for that matter, would suspect of illegal activity.

This is why I urged the FITE office's public information officer to put out press releases about these convictions and jail sentences. Admittedly, I pushed this idea with such intensity that I was banned from saying "press release" at our weekly meetings because there was some resistance to this change in policy. I knew that if information on these cases were made readily available, law enforcement, the justice system and even news reporters would pay attention. Business owners may not be that interested in a teenager who stole a car, but they would take the time to read about the "nice" office manager who stole about a million dollars from her dental practice employer.

Plus, there was the "Google effect" to consider. If embezzlers had press releases tied to their names, then business owners Googling potential employees would have access to pertinent information. This would allow employers to make more informed hiring decisions and better protect their livelihoods. In the end, my colleagues agreed with me and the sheriff's office started featuring convicted embezzlers in the quarterly newsletter.

I've given my presentation about detection and prevention of embezzlement many times over the years. And I'm still surprised by the scale of this problem based on the questions that participants ask during and after the sessions. It seems that everyone knows someone who has been a victim of embezzlement or knows someone who was an embezzler.

Of course, most people can't relate to the criminal fraud cases covered by the media, like the Bernie Madoff scandal and the infamous Enron debacle. However, most people can relate to the office manager ripping off the local chiropractor, the mother embezzling from a youth soccer program or a municipal clerk stealing to support a gambling habit. These types of suspects live in our communities. Their kids go to school with our kids. They're average people who, for one reason or another, crossed the line into criminal behavior. Their stories are featured prominently in this book to help you better understand, identify and prevent embezzlement.

Whether you are a small business owner, accountant, auditor, taxpayer or parent, this book will further your knowledge about embezzlement. After all, no one is invulnerable to financial fraud. It's simply a byproduct of our society, which requires that we not only trust other people but also businesses and systems.

By the way, falling victim to an embezzlement scheme absolutely does not mean you're foolish or a lousy businessperson. It means that someone took advantage of you financially or with regard to your assets. Trust me, I too have been indirectly swindled by an embezzler. The irrigation district for my area of the county was embezzled to the tune of $200,000. Unfortunately, the alleged suspect killed herself when she realized management had caught on to her thievery. That is a red-collar crime. A red-collar crime is defined as when the alleged criminal uses violence to escape detection of the financial crime or to escape prosecution or jail.

With the type of embezzlement I'm focusing on in this book being such a study in human behavior, maybe my fourth act career should be fraud therapist.

Before we move on, I should clarify two terms I've started using: embezzlement and fraud. Embezzlement and fraud have slightly different meanings. The crime of embezzlement involves withholding someone's or a business' assets (e.g., money) dishonestly and later claiming ownership of those assets. Fraud is intentionally cheating an individual or business for money or goods. Embezzlement is committed through fraudulent acts. Most of what I cover in this book falls into the embezzlement category—someone is committing a type of theft.

Importantly, I want to introduce you to the name for the category of embezzlement at the heart of this book. It's *pink-collar crime*. To explain this, I'll use a quote from when I was interviewed for an article in *Forbes* magazine.[1]

> Pink-collar crime involves low- to mid-level employees, primarily women, who steal from the workplace. The concept is about position, not gender. Women hold 90% of all bookkeeping jobs. These are the positions where money moves through business. The people in these roles know the accounting and office systems better than most. They see every dollar that goes through the business, from the CEO's expenses to vendor payments.

We'll further explore the range of pink-collar crimes throughout this book, based on my experience working in this field and real cases. My hope is that it will help you better understand the nature of these crimes and the people who commit such acts.

Introduction

Today's Pink-Collar Criminals

What do you think of when you hear the word *crime*? A physical assault? An armed robbery? A grisly murder? You're not alone. Most people equate crimes with violence because that's what they see every time they turn on the evening news, binge-watch the latest true-crime documentary or catch the opening of a Law & Order TV show rerun. The more sensational and ghastly the crime, the more coverage it receives.

Of course, just because the media would have you believe there's a serial killer lurking around every corner doesn't make it so. According to the FBI's *2019 Semiannual Uniform Crime Report*, the violent crime rate in the U.S. dropped 49 percent from 1993 to 2017.[2] For many of us then, the streets are safer than our office suites. The FBI reports that the cost of street crime is estimated to be $15 billion compared to estimates of $1 trillion for white-collar crime. The average person is much more likely to fall victim to a financial crime—which has increased to date—than a violent one, according to statistics from local, state and federal law enforcement.

It's common knowledge that men commit more crimes than women, particularly violent crimes such as murder. Ninety (90) percent of homicides are perpetrated by men.[3] Still, many people are probably unaware that this gender gap disappears when considering criminal fraud cases. The fact is that women constitute 57 percent of persons involved in embezzlement, according the *2013 Marquet Report on Embezzlement.*[4]

I want to emphasize here and now that men commit plenty of pink-collar crimes. However, most of the crimes that I describe in this book were perpetrated by women because they dominate the pink-collar crime category. I touch on that in more detail later in this book.

So who are these pink-collar criminals? According to TV shows, novels and sensationalistic news media, they are young, cunning seductresses who use their physical beauty and charms to manipulate men's hearts and bank accounts. Of course, real life doesn't always imitate art. Most embezzlers are middle-aged and stealing from their employers and community organizations. Forget about the sexy swindler and clever impersonator.

Instead, pay attention to Sharon the bookkeeper, Nancy the office manager, Tom the municipal clerk and Linda the PTA board member. After all, they live among us. These people are our friends and neighbors. They're exceptionally unexceptional, with stable families, modest incomes and often no criminal history of embezzlement. This also is the fastest growing group of criminals in the U.S. The fact is that women's prisons are filling up with Main Street women. The question is, why? In part, it's about the downside of economic opportunity.

Though women have yet to attain full gender equality, journalist Tom Brokaw focused on the measurable economic progress of the feminist movement, declaring this the "century of women" on MSNBC's Morning Joe[5] TV show in 2018. He noted that more females around the world are, "…taking [leadership] jobs that they were cut out of before."

This means, with more and more women joining the workforce, embezzlement statistics will continue to rise. This isn't because women are inherently deceitful or more calculating than men—though I'm sure there are those who would say otherwise—but because of the jobs they occupy. Women have direct access to money and financial records through pink-collar professions like bookkeeping, clerical work and bank telling. Still, we tend to overlook this particular consequence because we all are so preoccupied with the social effects of female employment on families and children.

People are predisposed to categorical thinking: good or bad, right or wrong, friend or foe. Unfortunately for our shortcut-loving brains, female embezzlers don't resemble prototypical criminals. Therefore, it's all of our responsibility to see these female professionals who choose to commit crimes for the victimizers they are, not the victims we expect them to be. We must overcome our unconscious biases and remember that affability and criminality are not mutually exclusive.

That said, most working women will not become fraud statistics, even though they have the potential to do so. And the purpose of this book is not to produce paranoid readers and conspiracy theorists. Though, would I tell you if it were? No, in all seriousness, my hope is that you feel confident and secure after reading this book, fully equipped to identify pink flags and implement safeguards to prevent crimes. Or, at least, take the appropriate steps should you or a loved one fall victim to a pink-collar crime.

PART ONE

Understanding How Honest People Steal

Chapter 1: Pink-Collar Versus White-Collar Crime

To be trusted is a greater compliment than to be loved.

—George MacDonald, author and minister

Most people know the term white-collar crime, which calls to mind images of preppy hedge fund managers and greedy investors on Wall Street who get caught cheating the system.

The poster boy for white-collar crime is none other than former financier Bernie Madoff. He's going to die in prison for running the largest Ponzi scheme in history. Specifically, Madoff defrauded thousands of clients to the tune of $64.8 billion by promising steady returns on their investments with little to no risk.[6]

To carry off his scheme, he had some of his longtime employees create fake brokerage statements and trade confirmations to sell his lie. The reality was that behind the scenes Madoff was simply using the money from incoming investors to pay off existing investors. That's a Ponzi scheme. His operation continued without a hitch until the stock market crashed in 2008, at which point more investors demanded their returns than Madoff could afford to pay.

Another interesting story about Bernie Madoff is when he told his assistant, Eleanor Squillari, about one of his clients who was embezzled by his assistant.[7] Squillari recalls an unusually prescient conversation she had with Madoff, after that assistant had been arrested. "You know, [he] has to take some responsibility for this," Madoff told Squillari. "He should have been keeping an eye on his personal finances. That's why I've always had Ruth watching the books. Nothing gets by Ruth." Squillari says she was surprised when he added, "Well, you know what happens is, it starts out with you taking a little bit, maybe a few hundred, a few thousand. You get comfortable with that, and before you know it, it snowballs into something big."

It seems to me that Bernie could have just been a regular pink-collar criminal except for the fact he had created opportunities to steal on a much larger scale. Of course, this is just one example of white-collar crime. For a more comprehensive understanding, we have to go back a few decades.

The term white-collar crime was coined in 1939 by Edwin Sutherland, the former president of the American Sociological Society. By the way, this group is now referred to as the American Sociological Association because, and I'm just making an educated guess here, ASA is a more tasteful acronym than ASS.

Back to Sutherland and white-collar crime. He defined this type of crime as "…committed by a person of respectability and high social status in the course of his occupation."[8] Sutherland's decision to emphasize the perpetrator's social standing was truly groundbreaking at the time. After all, most people had assumed that aristocrats were above breaking the law and that criminality was exclusive to members of the lower class with mental and social challenges.

Sutherland was a trailblazer who changed the way people viewed crime, but it's worth pointing out just how narrow his scope of focus was. You see, in fixating on offenders in positions of power, Sutherland effectively overlooked women who, in the late 1930s and early 1940s, typically held low-level clerical and service jobs. While they certainly didn't have the workplace opportunities to engage in white-collar crimes like insider trading, insurance fraud and Ponzi schemes, women still managed to steal from their employers. This is why Kathleen Daly, Ph.D. popularized the term "pink-collar crime" in 1989 in *Criminology Magazine*.[9]

So what exactly is a pink-collar crime? Well, much like its white-collared predecessor, Daly's term describes a nonviolent, financially-motivated crime. However, in this case, the perpetrator is operating from a position of limited power—think bookkeeper as opposed to CFO.

Did you notice that I used gender-neutral subjects in the previous sentence? That's because contrary to popular belief, men also can be pink-collar criminals. The label refers to the perpetrator's occupation, not gender. It's the offense, not the offender that's most relevant.

Just look at Rodolfo Olivas, an accountant in West Melbourne, Florida, who was arrested in 2018 for stealing from his longtime employer, Hills Inc.[10] Police said Olivas used business checks, unauthorized credit cards and multiple bank accounts to steal approximately $1.3 million over the course of seven years. Olivas' theft was a prototypical pink-collar crime because of his job as a bookkeeper, the methods he used to embezzle and the fact that he stole repeatedly over an extended period of time.

That said, Olivas is actually the exception, not the rule. While some pink-collar criminals are men, the majority are women. Why? Because the majority of pink-collar workers are women.

Just consider these statistics from the U.S. Department of Labor for the year of 2016.[11] Women accounted for the following:

- 94.6% of secretaries and administrative assistants.
- 90.7% of payroll and timekeeping clerks.
- 89% of billing and posting clerks.
- 88.5% of bookkeeping, accounting and auditing clerks.
- 81.7% of bank tellers.

What do these positions have in common, other than being female-dominated? For starters, they guarantee direct access to money on a regular basis, often with minimal supervision. What's more, they're typically underpaid with limited prospects for upward mobility. In this way, pink-collar jobs give occupants the opportunity as well as the incentive to steal. So is it any wonder that aside from prostitution, the majority of female arrests are for minor property crimes, such as larceny-theft, fraud, forgery and embezzlement?[12]

Background on pink-collar crime

In 1975, Freda Adler, Ph.D. authored *Sisters in Crime: The Rise of the New Female Criminal*, a highly controversial book in which she hypothesized that female crime rates would increase as a direct result of the women's liberation movement.[13] Before the defining social movement of the 1970s, a large percentage of women were not in the business workforce. So, according to Adler, that meant they lacked the opportunity and desire to commit crimes.

Still, the fight for equality translated to more women abandoning the domestic sphere in favor of the economic world. Adler said that in order to succeed in the latter, liberated women were adopting masculine behaviors including crime participation. She appeared in over 300 media events. But for the most part, all she got was backlash from criminologists and feminists alike. The former criticized, among other things, her methodology and interpretation of statistics. The latter worried that antifeminists would use her research to bolster their argument that women should stay in the home.

I reached out to Adler, who was kind enough to make time for an interview during which we discussed her seminal work. Early on in our conversation, she informed me that if she had known just how much pushback *Sisters in Crime* would receive, she may never have written the book that changed the way people viewed women and crime in the first place.

That said and fortunately for the field of criminology, Adler's conscience propelled her to publish her theory. After all, she wanted the public to be aware of the darker side of the women's liberation movement, from rising female incarceration rates to the ill-equipped criminal justice system. Adler told me that only four percent of the system's funding was allocated for women at the time. Her findings earned little support from her fellow criminologists, many of whom believed there were other explanations for the rise in female crime between the 1960s and early 1970s. But that doesn't change the fact that she helped establish female criminality as a valid field of study.

Before 1975, there was very little in the way of research or academic writing on female criminality. Early-20th-century theorists focused predominantly on male criminality. The few who actually considered female criminality were influenced by the dominant view of the time. Namely, believing that human behavior was deterministic or innate. These scientists claimed that individual biological and psychological characteristics, as opposed to collective social or economic conditions, were the main cause of female criminality.[14]

For example, Italian physician and criminologist Cesare Lombroso believed that most women weren't capable of committing crimes due to their inherent weakness and intellectual inferiority to men. He referred to criminal women as "biologically dysfunctional."[15] Wow, I'm sure he had a healthy relationship with his mother!

Speaking of psychoanalysis, Austrian neurologist Sigmund Freud echoed this sentiment, stating that women were destined to be wives and mothers—not criminals—because of their physical and mental limitations.[16] Unlike Lombroso though, Freud believed that female offenders were acting out of revenge for not having penises. Specifically, he theorized that all young girls desire penises and when that desire isn't met, some fall into neuroticism and adopt more masculine characteristics. I even hesitate to include this about Freud because I was so horrified when I read it. Like the old Virginia Slims cigarette ad touted, "We've come a long way, baby!"

Situated within this larger context, Adler's work was nothing short of revolutionary as she argued that criminality is a product of social, not just biological forces. Today, the social pressures on women are enormous. According to the Pew Research Foundation, women were the primary breadwinners in 11 percent of U.S. households with children under the age of 18 in 1960 compared to 40 percent in 2014.[17]

Yet despite the rising economic standing of women roughly "…seven-in-ten adults say it is very important for a man to be able to support a family financially," while just three-in-ten adults say the same about women, according to that Pew research. Clearly, though much has changed since the publication of *Sisters in Crime*, including a marked increase in women's educational attainment, labor-force participation and earnings has stayed the same. Okay, I'm looking at you… gender stereotypes.

A study published in *Psychology of Women Quarterly* found that gender stereotypes have remained relatively stable from 1983 to 2014.[18] Specifically, men continue to be associated with traits like action oriented and independence, while women are often seen as warm and concerned with the welfare of others. With that in mind, it's hardly surprising that the majority of managerial positions are occupied by men and the service industry is dominated by women. Adler touched on this discrepancy during our interview, noting that there isn't a female Madoff and there never will be until more women are in positions of power.

For now, the closest we have to a female Madoff is Elizabeth Holmes, the founder and former CEO of health-tech startup Theranos. She was indicted on conspiracy and wire fraud charges in 2018. She allegedly mislead investors, corporate partners, doctors and patients about the capabilities of her company's blood-testing technology.[19] Holmes is a textbook white-collar criminal, using her social respectability and position of power to execute financial crimes. However, her $700 million fraud scheme—funds she raised from investors—pales in comparison to

Madoff's $64.8 billion Ponzi scheme. Yes, even in crime, women face a glass ceiling!

Another female white-collar criminal who made headlines in 2018 was Nancy Jackson Carroll, the former owner of a title company in Southlake, Texas. She was ordered to pay over $8.6 million in restitution for stealing clients' funds.[20] In a recorded phone call with her mother, Carroll referred to herself as the "Millennium Mobster" and suggested that Reese Witherspoon should play her in a true-crime movie. She even tried to contact the publisher of *The Wolf of Wall Street* about a book deal. Was that an indication of an unpretentious, remorseful person? In that conversation with her mother, Carroll can be heard laughing about her crimes, stating that she wouldn't be prosecuted because they were only white-collar charges. She was sentenced to 10 years in prison on January 3, 2018.

Believe it or not, Carroll's belief that fraud is a relatively minor offense is pretty common. Many people assume that white-collar crimes are victimless despite their devastating consequences.

Certainly no one would claim that the Madoff case was a victimless crime. Take the example of Steve Heimoff, a wine writer and critic in California. He had set aside money for retirement that was unknowingly invested in Madoff's enterprise and was suddenly gone.[21] Prior to 2008, he had never heard of Bernie Madoff, yet he was among the many victims of the now-infamous fraudster. It later came out that Stanley Chais, a local fund manager to whom Heimoff had entrusted his money, had been quietly serving as one of the largest "feeders" to Madoff's Ponzi scheme. Heimoff lost $2 million and, at the age of 62, was forced to refinance his condominium and significantly reduce his spending.

Other Madoff victims were forced to sell their homes, declare bankruptcy or put off retirement.[22] Many died waiting for restitution and at least four people connected to the case committed suicide. I've spoken with Harry Markopolos who investigated Madoff. He told me that many others committed suicide but never made the news for their deaths tied to the loss of their money. If that's not enough, Madoff's crimes cost a variety of charities and hospitals millions of dollars, forcing some organizations to close their doors forever. In this way, the effects of fraud are not limited to the individual but are also felt at the organizational, community and societal levels.

The FBI and the Association of Certified Fraud Examiners (ACFE) estimate that white-collar crime costs the U.S. between $300 and $660 billion every year.[23] Five percent of business revenue is estimated to be lost every year due to fraud. Of course, it's difficult to pinpoint an exact amount because so many of these types of offenses go unreported. A public survey on white-collar crime found that only one-third of victims notify the authorities.[24] Why? Typically businesses want to avoid negative publicity and individuals feel immense shame for being duped. Fraud and embezzlement are a little like porn in that far more people watch it than would ever admit it.

I recently attended a holiday party with a diverse group of people. The one thing they all had in common was, you guessed it, having been embezzled or knowing someone who had been a victim. It's the relatable crime. I call it the dirty little secret in business. Think "Six Degrees of Kevin Bacon"—you know, that game where you try to find the shortest path of connections between an individual or random actor and Kevin Bacon? But in this case, there's only one degree of separation.

When people find out what I do, they take stock of their surroundings and start speaking in hushed tones, "I want to tell you what happened to me." From holiday parties to networking events, I've had many people pour their hearts out to me.

Embezzlement is everywhere there's trust

Even though embezzlement is very common, most people are preoccupied with street crimes not suite crimes. They have security companies monitor their homes for burglars and hire watchmen to protect their warehouses. But what do they do for their bank accounts? Maybe they balance their checkbooks or add longer passwords to their sensitive accounts.

Still, many business owners think that just because a person has no criminal history or is the daughter of their favorite golf buddy, that qualifies her to be their office manager or bookkeeper. Spoiler alert: It doesn't. As I regularly tell my clients, trust is not an internal control.

Being swindled is bad, but I would argue that being swindled by someone you trusted is worse. This is one of the key differences between white- and pink-collar crime. You see, perpetrators of the former tend to have minimal interaction with their victims. An embezzler is most likely closer to the victim than a white-collar criminal. Whereas Eugene Soltes argues in his article "The psychology of white-collar criminals" for *The Atlantic*, it's that psychological and physical distance that enables white-collar criminals to do what they do."[25] Think about it. If you don't know the majority of the people that your decisions affect, as is the case with many business executives, then you don't have to think about the harm you're inflicting or witness any victim reactions.

Meanwhile, pink-collar criminals usually develop a deep level of trust and intimacy with their targets. They don't just work with their victims but often socialize after hours too. I can't tell you how many stories I've read in which the victim of a pink-collar crime describes the perpetrator as an honorary family member. They say, "I trusted her with everything" are sentiments I come across daily. The devastation from this is immeasurable. It's the worst part of the deception. Money is replaceable, but the breach of trust is far more devastating.

Consider this quote from Jed Block, the president and CEO of Goodwill Industries of North Central Wisconsin, Inc., in which he details his reaction to the news that a longtime employee embezzled upwards of $500,000 over a seven-year period. He said, "On a personal level, I felt shame, embarrassment and anger. I also experienced a profound sense of loss of innocence and a challenge to my fundamental capacity to trust.

Before the embezzlement was discovered, I was an ardent fan of the employee who committed the fraud against us."[26]

If an employee's betrayal can spark such powerful emotions, just imagine what a spouse's betrayal can do. One woman, who spoke anonymously with *The Week's* Nora Zelevansky in 2013, recounted how her now ex-husband's embezzlement landed her in jail.[27] The story was that he convinced her to put her name on his company's checks, arguing that the appearance of female management would give him minority status, which could lead to more funding down the road. She agreed, mostly out of fear, as he was emotionally abusive. It wasn't until several years later that she discovered his embezzlement scheme—the same day she was arrested. She had unknowingly been signing, endorsing and depositing checks for an illegal business. And since she couldn't prove that she wasn't in on the fraud, she ended up accepting a plea deal.

The person she had built a life with had just changed her life irrevocably. She went from making over $100,000 a year as a recruiter to having a criminal record, being responsible for half of her ex's debt—a cool $1 million—declaring bankruptcy and relying on food stamps and social services to get by. In her own words, she will "…have to pay for the rest of…[her] life: financially, emotionally, psychologically. And so…[will her] daughter, who is an innocent party."

I recently worked on several theft cases in which the employer's spouse was the suspect. The first two involved dentists who hired their spouses to be their office managers. In both cases, the pink-collar spouse embezzled from the practice. Clearly, these betrayals were emotionally and financially taxing for the dentists. Then, to add insult to injury, the dentists struggled to get justice. More often than not, prosecutors won't get involved in theft cases when there's a divorce and/or civil prosecution going on. It's just too messy. There's commingling of funds in personal and business accounts. And of course, there's the higher level of emotions when you add the divorce to a theft. In my experience, the only people who win in these cases are the divorce attorneys.

Speaking of the financial impacts of relationships going wrong, use caution when filing joint tax returns. A small-business owner that I worked with had to re-file his taxes and make additional payments because his deductions and expenses were off by several hundred thousand dollars. How is that possible? Turns out his then-wife had been embezzling from the business. Including taxes, interest and penalties, he owed the Internal Revenue Service (IRS) around $100,000. You read that right: Taxes are due on stolen money. A number like that can be the demise of a small business.

According to a family law attorney I spoke with, the theft of funds is called "marital waste" and something that judges don't really take into account. So, if you think you can just deduct that loss from your settlement, don't be too sure. Additionally, if the funds are deposited into a joint account, then it's nearly impossible to prove that you didn't know they were stolen.

In that regard, Rick Jacobsen is a lucky man. When his wife, Tina Lemmens, was arrested for stealing around $500,000 from the blood bank where she worked as an accountant, Jacobsen was expected to pay upwards of $100,000 in taxes on the embezzled money.[28] He had been unaware of his wife's crimes, but because the couple had filed joint tax returns, he was liable for the unreported income. Jacobsen ended up filing an appeal. While he got the majority of the sum relieved, he was still responsible for $18,000. No one should count on that happening. It's a long, hard road to battle. After all, you're taking on the federal government, a system with practically unlimited resources.

Now before anyone confronts a spouse with unwarranted suspicions, it's important to realize that many financial crimes are preventable. The key is to remove the opportunity to commit those crimes.

Whether it's a pink-collar or white-collar crime, a crime is a crime. But as you now can see, pink-collar crimes and the people who commit them can seem to operate more easily under the public's attention radar even after discovery and prosecution. Crimes usually stem from plenty of opportunities and rationalizations, not the headline garnering drivers of greed or all out criminal intent. Throw out your stereotypes of the typical "bad guy" and realize that anyone can cross the line and embezzle from a business, given the opportunity.

Pink-collar prevention tips:

- One of the easiest and lowest cost ways to prevent employee theft is to have your business's bank statements mailed directly to your home, check your statements online and segregate accounting duties as much as possible. This means the employee who receives the money shouldn't also deposit it. By adopting these habits you will send a very clear message to anyone who has the potential to rip you off that you are paying attention.

- Passwords are like toothbrushes. Don't share them. There are so many reasons not to share personal passwords for internal or external financial accounts. Too often, people are in a hurry and just quickly want an associate to add something to a file or a report. But your password is your digital fingerprint and it links you to the account activity, legal or illegal. You don't want to be accused of something you didn't do, such as a money transfer, vendor payment, payroll change, etc., just because you shared your password.

- To prevent spousal theft, take the time to sit down with your partner and go through the finances. Where are your investments? What are your savings? Are there any debts? Do your accounts balance? Are there changes in your partner's behavior that are concerning? Are you spending noticeably more money in your day-to-day life? Going to the fancy steak house instead of Olive Garden? Talk it all out, together.

Chapter 2: The Fraud Triangle

Fraud is not an accounting problem; it's a social phenomenon.

—Joseph Wells, founder and Chairman of the
Board, Association of Certified Fraud Examiners

I know what you're thinking, reading this chapter title: Geometry connected to fraud. Really? But stay with me. The *fraud triangle* is a model that explains why and how people commit workplace fraud. Criminologists Donald Cressey and Edwin Sutherland developed the concept in the 1950s, but the term fraud triangle didn't actually appear until the publication of Joseph Wells' book, *Occupational Fraud and Abuse*, in 1997.[29]

The fraud triangle consists of—you guessed it—three parts: (1) pressure, (2) rationalization and (3) opportunity. Each point is defined below. I bring this up because in order to avoid being victimized by pink-collar criminals, you must first understand how they operate.

1. **Pressure** - the perceived need—often financial, but not always—to commit fraud.
2. **Rationalization** - the mindset that justifies fraudulent behavior.
3. **Opportunity** - the circumstances that allow fraud to occur, typically when internal controls are weak or nonexistent.

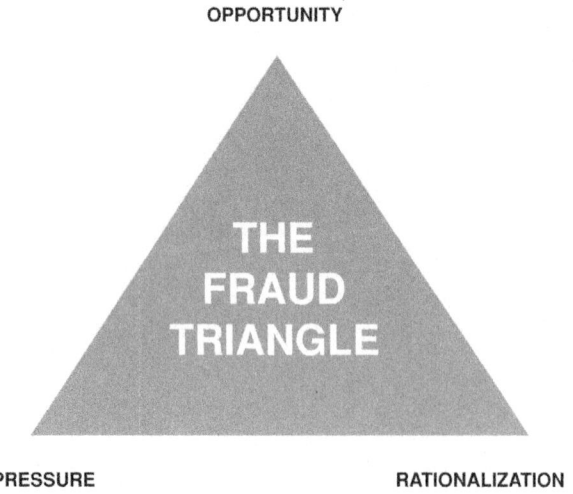

The only factor with the fraud triangle that an employer can fully control is opportunity. But don't think a business can't influence an employee's rationalization. An administrative assistant may earn $1 million per year in salary, but if she needs and feels deserving of $2 million, then she may steal if given the opportunity. I've had many clients proudly share that they pay their staff above the going wage rate. That's great, but whether or not the employee considers that *enough* is a separate matter. In today's digital age, where upward social comparisons and FOMO (fear of missing out) are pervasive, everyone has a different idea of what, exactly, is enough.

The following are some real-life examples of occupational pink-collar crime, which I'll examine through the lens of the fraud triangle.

Under Pressure

"Nobody can understand the devastation we are going through."[30] That's a quote from Paul Marinaccio Sr., a 66-year-old Italian man who founded a successful construction company after immigrating to the U.S. as a teenager. He said this at the sentencing of his longtime bookkeeper for embezzling over $700,000.

An article from the *Buffalo News* painted Marinaccio as a caring boss who paid his employees well, providing health insurance and bonuses, and even offering to help, "…pay their mortgages and car loans." So it came as a shock to him when he learned that Debora Gramza, a family friend whom he, "…trusted with everything," had been forging checks for nearly five years.

Why was a job with great benefits not enough for Gramza? According to her attorney, Gramza's son was abusing drugs and the bookkeeper believed she could keep him out of jail by giving him money—as in responding to the *pressure* of her situation. Did Marinaccio know that Gramza's son had a drug problem? I'm not sure. Of course, not everyone who has a sick or drug-addicted child will steal. Remember, they certainly won't steal if the opportunity doesn't present itself.

In a similar story, a former bookkeeper for a school district in Bangor, Maine, was indicted for embezzling upwards of $200,000 to help her drug-addicted son. Yvonne Mitchell, the bookkeeper, said she stole the money to cover her son's living expenses and addiction treatment.[31] However it quickly came to light that, "…she also used the money to pay her daughter's out-of-state college tuition and her own living expenses."

Mitchell's initial decision to steal may very well be traced back to the costs and pressure associated with her son's substance abuse problem. Still, it's important to understand that she also used him to rationalize her fraudulent behavior.

As you'll see in the next example cases, pink-collar criminals can justify just about anything—to themselves, at least—when pressure and opportunity knock.

A Large Dose of Rationalization

Shannon Nagle was a well-paid office manager, taking home $110,000 per year, and she decided to steal from her younger sister's health clinic in 2010. The story reads like a soap opera.

Nagle started embezzling from her sister's medical practice in Aspen, Colorado, shortly after her promotion to office manager. She used clinic credit cards to purchase groceries and other small, personal items. Why? Because according to an article from the *Aspen Times*, she felt "anger and resentment" toward her sister mainly over shared real estate transactions.[32] That was her rationalization for theft.

In this case, Nagle's fraudulent activity didn't stop there, as she began binge shopping in 2014. Her rationalization this time around? An eating disorder and other health problems. Over time, Shannon Nagle racked up more and more purchases, mostly for herself but also for her immediate family. Well, maybe not for her sister Melinda. For example, when one of Shannon's daughters started to excel at horseback riding, she had the clinic cover all of the associated costs. Maybe not surprisingly, horses are a pink flag for pink-collar crime.

Additionally, according to the affidavit, "…airplane flights and in-flight charges were purchased using the card, along with lengthy expensive hotel stays and various vacation charges. …Also noted were charges for plastic surgery and cosmetics. Lastly, many personal charges [were made], such as car repair, car registration, gas, music, horse boarding, various saddles and accessories for horses and other pets, and miscellaneous grocery shopping."

The judge in the case stated that Shannon Nagle "…took advantage of a lapse in attention to the system." That addressed the defendant's opportunity to steal, but what may be more interesting was her knack for rationalizing her actions. The affidavit also stated that Nagle was "angry and in denial," often feeling "unappreciated at work" because she didn't receive raises like other employees. On top of that, the defendant claimed, "…that (Melinda) Nagle and (her business partner) believed she wasn't worth her salary."

Another interesting story involving rationalization is about Gary Foster. Foster stole $22 million from Citibank over a period of six years.[33] What's amazing is the rationalization that started this embezzlement. Foster saw that someone who reported to him earned $10,000 more than he did. He was devastated and disappointed. He felt betrayed. This is where rationalization came in. He loved his job at Citibank. It took him almost two years to decide to steal after seeing his subordinate was earning more than he. But once he started, he did it with aplomb. Buying luxury cars, houses and traveling the world were just a few of the ways he spent the stolen money. Foster actually left Citibank before he was caught.

The other part of the story regarded Foster's boss, Peter C. Orlandi. Orlandi discovered the fraud as part of an audit.[34] One month later, Orlandi says, he was summoned to Citibank's Manhattan headquarters and told he "…was terminated due to a lack of leadership regarding the Gary Foster situation." Orlandi claimed that he turned in Foster, an activity protected under whistle-blower laws, including Sarbanes-Oxley and Dodd-Frank Acts. "Orlandi's protected activity was a contributing factor in Citibank's adverse employment action against him, which constituted discrimination," Orlandi said.

Supervisors who attend my trainings truly believe they hire good, honest people. When someone ends up stealing on their watch, often it reflects poorly on their leadership and supervision. Orlandi's story is not the first case of a superior being terminated for not managing "effectively" and it certainly won't be the last.

While such rationalizations don't make stealing acceptable, business owners need to understand that in the eyes of a pink-collar criminal, they do. Remember, opportunity is the easiest part of the fraud triangle to control. However, you can influence rationalization. What are the other lesson learned from this sad story? Trust your employees, but always verify information about them and the work they do for you even if they are family members.

Opportunity

In 2014, *Today Show* correspondent Jeff Rossen conducted an investigative news segment on parents embezzling from school booster clubs. The report detailed a case in Virginia. The treasurer of a marching band's booster club, Kimberly Compitello, stole nearly $14,000 over the course of one year.[35] In case you were wondering, yes, her own child was a member of the band at the time. Compitello definitely had the opportunity to get away with this theft for some time.

Rossen also cited an Ohio case in which a man stole approximately $439,000 from an athletic booster club over an eight-year span. He had the same opportunity as Compitello due to direct access to organization's funds. As I've said, pink-collar crime is not gender specific.

Such stories come as no surprise to me, as opportunities for fraud arise all the time for organizations. Just the other day I read about a so-called "incredible" volunteer who was arrested for stealing from a local high school near my home in Portland, Oregon.[36] Cindy Schorn, a well-known volunteer for the Banks School District, pocketed some of the cash she collected from the opportunity of selling tickets at school basketball games.

These thefts weren't discovered during an audit. You see, most booster clubs don't have basic financial controls in place, let alone audits. Schorn's theft was only discovered when administrators watched surveillance footage of a disagreement between students, which just so happened to catch the longtime volunteer taking money out of a school cash box. How long had this been going on? The school district had no idea. Schorn had been a volunteer for eight years and according to the county sheriff's spokesperson, "…[s]he had access to money in a lot of ways."

Every week I hear different variations of the same story. A dedicated volunteer has stolen from the local soccer team, jazz band or cheerleading squad. The opportunity presents itself because parent volunteers are seen as moral, honest and helpful. This blind trust protects the wolves in sheep's clothing. Booster officers and school administrators are often reluctant to implement the internal controls necessary to prevent embezzlement out of fear that volunteers will feel like their integrity is being questioned.

With that in mind, one parent—who may not even have a background in finance—is typically dubbed club treasurer, single-handedly carrying out all of the financial responsibilities from depositing cash to reconciling the checkbook. With no oversight to speak of, is it any wonder that some club funds may end up in a volunteer's personal wallet or checking account? Now if someone quickly volunteers to be treasurer I might be suspicious. After all, it's a thankless job and most volunteers have no interest in doing it. That is unless they know they can steal and likely get away with it.

While no two booster-club embezzlement cases are exactly alike, the perpetrators of these crimes do tend to share certain characteristics. For starters, most of them are women. Volunteerism data from the Bureau of Labor Statistics shows that regardless of age, race and education level, women volunteer more than men.[37] Therefore, it makes sense that more women steal from these types of organizations than men because of access and opportunity.

Additionally, volunteers convicted of fraud are predominantly middle-aged. This isn't surprising, what with the positive association between parenthood and volunteering and the fact that over 30 percent of Americans between the ages of 40 and 50 volunteer, according to the Bureau of Labor Statistics. What's more, this type of criminal is also known for embezzling relatively small amounts of money at a time, which accumulate over years without detection.

That was exactly the case with a Wisconsin school bookkeeper named Jessica Warner-Reed.[38] She was sentenced to two years in prison in 2016 for stealing more than $300,000 over the course of nine years. Warner-Reed was responsible for collecting and depositing money from 140 student clubs and teams, making this yet another school theft case where opportunity was not managed.

So how did this nearly decade-long embezzlement scheme begin? With a meager $10.00. Specifically, Warner-Reed took that money out of one of the school district's bank accounts in 2007. However, when no one noticed the missing funds, the bookkeeper opted to continue her fraudulent behavior, which only escalated with time. When it comes to occupational theft, no dollar amount is too small to ignore.

Another example of an individual taking advantage of an opportunity was with the office manager of a longtime friend of mine. My friend was watching the books for her family's business. She noticed that the office manager, Faye, had bought some personal items with a company credit card while shopping at Costco for office supplies. My friend informed her brother, the CEO, about the purchases which he quickly dismissed as "petty." He was certain Faye would pay them back and never do it again.

Several years later, Faye was caught embezzling approximately $500,000 from that employer. Neither my friend nor her brother was aware that Faye had a gambling problem. However, that doesn't change the fact that they should have fired her after the initial theft. I'm sure my friend's Thanksgiving dinner with the family wasn't all that festive.

Embezzlement can and often does tear families apart. The finger pointing starts almost immediately. I know another family business with two brothers who were victims of embezzlement. One brother pointed the finger at the other brother and vice versa. Who was to blame? It's hard to say definitively. But I do know it caused heartache and grief for the families.

It's easy to read the previous stories and think, "That won't happen to me." Business owners love to tell me about all of the financial safeguards they've implemented, such as: "I sign all of the checks" and "My accountant would find any fraud." While I applaud their efforts to reduce the chance for theft, the reality is that technology has created countless opportunities for employees to engage in fraud.

For example, one case during my time working for the Washington County Sheriff's Office in Hillsboro, Oregon involved a young woman named Tiffany who worked at a wine tasting room. When she quit— that's right, she was not fired—the owner noticed his business credit card bill included two purchases that were clearly personal. Angry, he called the Sheriff's Office to report a $400 theft.

So, you can imagine his shock and indignation when, a few months later, I informed him that Tiffany had actually made off with approximately $450,000. The owner hadn't looked at the refunds on his credit card account because according to him, there were no circumstances under which his business would issue a refund. He said, "They try the wine and if they like it, they buy it. If they don't like it, they don't buy it." Clearly, he had not been aware that Tiffany had the opportunity to process refunds to her personal credit cards. The odd thing was, he said he never liked her and was glad when she quit.

Out of all the victims I've come across, he has been the only one who told me that he or she didn't like the suspect. All of the other victims really did like their suspects right until they were caught.

Pink-collar prevention tips:
- The big takeaway here? Trust your gut! If your intuition says something isn't right, then think about which parts of the fraud triangle may be at play.

- Pay attention to what you see happening at the business. Listen to the conversations around the water cooler. Be aware of signs

reflecting your employees' lifestyles. Then, review your business or
bank accounts for opportunities to commit fraud. Are you
susceptible to vendor fraud or forgery? Are there any open bank
accounts that were supposed to be closed?

- Make sure you are aware of all bank accounts open under the
  company's or organization's name. To ensure the accounts at your
  bank or other banks are the proper ones or that obsolete ones have
  been closed, run your credit report annually and also have a good
  relationship with your banker. Always check in at least semi-annually
  or after any big financial event.

- Try to think like a criminal. After all, even longtime trusted
  employees are criminals when they steal. That's not to say you hired a
  criminal—perhaps you even hired a family member or friend—but
  when he or she spotted the opportunity, that was the starting point.
  Good people cross the line for many private, unpredictable reasons. I
  like to tell business owners that they are there to put guardrails in
  place to keep their employees honest.

- Use a mystery shopper/customer to check to see if cash sales policies
  are being followed. I had a potential client who was in the
  automobile repair business with a partner. He became concerned
  about the lack of profitability of the business. Originally, they agreed
  that no cash sales would be allowed by the business. He was certain
  his partner was skimming cash because the profits were low. Instead
  of hiring a forensic accountant, I advised him to try using a mystery
  shopper to test their cash sales policy. I suggested that he have a
  friend, unknown to his partner, go in for a service and attempt to pay
  with cash. If the co-owner took the cash, the other partner would
  have a basis for a deeper dive to investigate.

- If you want more information about thefts from youth sports,
  including preventative measures, check out The Center for Fraud
  Prevention at http://www.thefraudcenter.org.

PART TWO

How They Do It?

Chapter 3: Common Fraud Schemes

Fraud and deceit are anxious for your money. Be informed and prudent.

—John Andreas Widtsoe, Apostle,
The Church of Jesus Christ of Latter-day Saints

I'm not going to teach you how to steal. I will, however, describe some of the ways in which pink-collar criminals have committed their thievery. In nearly every case, it all boils down to the practices and habits of their employers. I've met many business owners who think they don't need to worry about employee theft because they, not their employees, sign the checks. Whenever I hear this, I usually just smile—a reaction that has been known to elicit some follow-up questions. Many times they listened to their accountants and got rid of their signature stamps, but that's only one defensive measure.

Too often they do have a few pre-signed checks locked away for emergencies. They say, "But that's okay, right? It definitely makes traveling easier." Again, I smile. Now it's my turn to ask some questions like, "Is there a ledger for those checks?" "Who has access to your safe?" and "When was the last time you verified that all of the checks were accounted for?"

There are many dozens of ways to embezzle money through a bank. A pink-collar criminal doesn't need a signed check to steal. In fact, according to the *2013 Marquet Report on Embezzlement*, an analysis of major embezzlement cases in the U.S., the most common fraud scheme revolves around the use of forged and unauthorized checks.[39] Cash skimming and vendor fraud also fall into this general category.

Check Writing/Tampering

Consider the case of Ryan Thorpe, the former treasurer for the town of Zeigler, Illinois. He pleaded guilty to embezzling over $321,000 by writing checks on the city's general account to himself.[40] It's hardly rocket science. Thorpe covered up his multiple thefts—quite literally—by using white-out fluid. The 44-year-old fraudster used an everyday office supply to remove his name from the check copies before writing in the names of city vendors and suppliers, making photocopies of the altered checks for the city's bank records, and shredding the originals.

Such check tampering is a form of vendor fraud. That's the manipulation of a company's payment systems for the perpetrator's personal gain. Other common examples of vendor fraud include billing schemes, bid rigging and kickbacks, each of which is described in more depth below.

More often than not, billing schemes involve the creation of fake vendors or the manipulation of real vendors' accounts to steal company funds. A recent example of the former took place in my home state of Oregon. Susan Tranberg, the ex-finance manager of a large timber company, was fired in January of 2019 for embezzling approximately $4.5 million from her employer of 42 years.[41]

Tranberg forged her coworkers' signatures to authorize payments to several fictitious vendors, including M.J. Miller and Margaret J. Miller, whom she named after her deceased mother. Maybe a way for her to honor the dead? She then used her mother's social security number and her own mailing address to get her hands on the payments made to the pseudo Millers.

I can't stress enough how easy it is to pull off these types of fraud schemes. An employee needs nothing more than a fake name and a PO box to get started. Susan Tranberg's thefts went undiscovered for at least 15 years. Her boss retired and she started stealing even more with her new position and authority. She kept her stolen funds under $10,000 each to avoid further scrutiny. When Tranberg was confronted, she offered her vacation balance to cover the loss. Even as a 42 year employee I don't think most employees have a $4.5 million vacation balance.

Another recent billing scheme took place in Maryland, but this time the perpetrator falsified invoices from real vendors to defraud two of her past employers.[42] Rebecca Jelfo worked as a marketing executive for both an airline and a hospitality company, approving marketing invoices from contract vendors. On multiple occasions, Jelfo submitted inflated invoices to her employers, which they paid. She would then order the vendors to remit payments to her personal credit card accounts. In less than two years, Jelfo stole upwards of $855,000, a hefty sum that she used to cover her personal debts and shop at luxury stores like Neiman Marcus and Saks Fifth Avenue. Jelfo was sentenced to over three years in prison on December 10, 2019, but she could have faced a maximum sentence of 20 years.

Bid Rigging

The billing schemes outlined above are relatively straightforward examples of vendor fraud in that they only required one perpetrator. Bid rigging, when an employee illegally helps a vendor obtain a contract that was supposed to result from competitive bidding, is more complicated since there typically are multiple perpetrators.

In 2012, Amber Crowder, a former District of Columbia school employee, colluded with her longtime friend, Shauna Brumfield, to ensure the latter won a $300,000 government contract.[43] Specifically, Crowder and Brumfield created a fake company to bid on a contract. It was a contract that Crowder was responsible for overseeing. She was a program manager in the Office of Special Education (OSE) of the District of Columbia Public Schools (DCPS).

To cover up this flagrant conflict of interest, Crowder's involvement in the company was never disclosed and Brumfield adopted an alias. Many qualified companies submitted bid proposals to OSE, but Crowder's intimate knowledge of the budget for the contract allowed Brumfield and her to beat out the competition, receiving approximately $300,000 from DCPS over the next two and a half years. The majority of those funds were transferred to Crowder's personal bank account. I do wonder if their friendship is strong enough to endure prison time, since the pair could spend a statutory maximum of 20 years behind bars.

Kickbacks

Another common type of vendor fraud that involves two or more perpetrators is a kickback. In this scheme, an employee is illegally compensated by a vendor for assisting in acts of fraud.

From October of 2010 through April of 2015, Palestine Ace colluded with her husband and an associate to embezzle over $2.7 million in a kickback scheme.[44] Ace was a senior vice president of Bank of America. They misappropriated funds from the bank's marketing budget to make fraudulent donations to multiple nonprofit organizations on behalf of Bank of America.

Palestine and her co-conspirators, Jonathan Ace and Brianna Alexis Forde, then demanded that the nonprofits return the bulk of the donations, claiming that if they didn't, Bank of America would pull any future funding. The organizations were instructed to return the funds to a specific Bank of America account, which Palestine Ace had access to, or they could write a check to Jonathan Ace or Forde. There's no question that the Aces profited the most from this scheme, although the $200,000 Forde received for her cooperation is nothing to sneeze at.

Credit Card Fraud

While all of the previous cases involve predominantly female defendants, the *2013 Marquet Report on Embezzlement* found that men are five times more likely to commit vendor fraud than women.[45] Why is that? In my experience, the data can be explained by the types of jobs men tend to hold. A mid-level manager is far more likely to be invited to sporting events and nice dinners than an administrative assistant. In this way, men often have more opportunities to form vendor relationships compared to women. This is a pattern that I expect to continue as we're living in the #MeToo era, which has likely made men more wary of socializing with women outside of work. Men may dominate vendor fraud schemes, but data show that women commit more credit card fraud.[46]

I heard fraudster Diann Cattani's story at the ACFE's 21st Annual Conference.[47] She was the ex-felon selected to close the event that year and the first pink-collar criminal I communicated with directly. Diann grew up in an upper-middle-class family and was an accomplished athlete who attended Brigham Young University on a volleyball scholarship. She was a good kid on the fast track until she wasn't. Diann ended up working for a company in the Southeastern U.S. where she was considered a rising star. She worked crazy hours, staying as long as it took to get everything done.

One Christmas, she decided to use her well-deserved vacation days to visit her family in Idaho. When she returned to work, she realized that the company travel agent had booked her personal tickets on the company card. It was after the holidays and her bills were mounting. Though, when she thought about it, colleagues from work had called and paged her throughout her trip. It really wasn't much of a vacation. That's when the rationalizations started creeping in. Diann told herself she would pay it back on the next pay period. Of course, if she had, you probably wouldn't be reading her story right now.

Over time, Diann repeatedly used company credit cards to pay her personal expenses. There always was a justification. The company Diann worked for had a contract with another company that capped the amount of work one vendor could provide. So what did Diann's company do? They simply created another company to get around that "ridiculous" rule. This is where tone at the top starts to play a role.

Diann was physically sick from all of the stress and guilt of being a thief. She then had what she refers to as the "Oprah Moment." She went home one afternoon and started watching an episode of The Oprah Winfrey Show in which Dr. Phil was a guest. He said you have to be true to yourself. Diann knew that she had to come clean to her boss. She didn't know the exact amount she had taken. Initially, she figured that she would be able to pay back the money, that she would walk away without a job but with her self-respect restored. The next thing she knew, she was having a baby while being incarcerated in a federal prison for women. Today, Diann is divorced and lives life with an asterisk. She can't coach her daughter's sports team due to her felony. Still, she managed to turn her life around. I remember looking at her and realizing it can happen to anyone.

This reminds me about a case I worked on in which the employee rebooked a trip. The woman, I'll call her Martha, decided to upgrade to first class and also add a stop in a vacation spot to meet friends. Her inappropriate charges were only caught because of the makeup she had charged on that company card. Martha's deceit was never ending yet she wasn't fired. She made justifications to her boss about how effective she was to be able to keep her job, even though the thefts had nothing to do with her effectiveness.

I interviewed Martha's boss and she was adamant it was just a "silly mistake." A month later she was caught violating the policies again but never was held accountable. Martha is still working for that company and I can't imagine she stopped justifying her thefts. She probably has just learned how better to hide her thefts. Ironically, Martha's boss was later let go and she was transferred to a new position.

When I first started working at the Sheriff's Office, one of my first cases was a homeowner's association (HOA) theft. The embezzler was responsible for maintenance at the condominium complex. He was provided with a company credit card to purchase maintenance and repair materials. His thievery started small. But it increased over time. Soon he had stolen approximately $40,000. You see, he had a child with special needs—a rationalization waiting to be used. When he went to Costco for the HOA, he would put a few items into the cart for his family. Eventually he bought bunk beds for his kids. The board didn't closely review any of his expenditures until it was too late. He ended up losing his job and was prosecuted.

After citing so many cases involving middle-aged perpetrators, I'm compelled to address the opportunities that millennials have because they are more computer savvy. This means that many more fraudulent acts are available to them, if they choose criminal lives.

For example, there was a very ambitious and technology savvy millennial CEO of Valor Federal Credit Union in Pennsylvania named Sean Jelen. He used various technologies and digital methods to steal hundreds of thousands of dollars from his credit union, according to the U.S. Department of Justice.[48]

Here's a list of just some of Jelen's crimes:

- Forged a fake service contract between Valor and a non-existent entity for $34,500 to pay off his credit card debt.

- Altered bank records to conceal his existing mortgage liability to obtain a $450,000 line of credit from Valor.

- Changed account records to have Valor double-pay his life insurance premium into his bank account to embezzle almost $140,000.

- Modified donation records to disguise a $25,000 golf tournament sponsorship at his alma mater as a donation to a local soup kitchen.

- And get this.… he even forged a severance contract to trigger millions of dollars in payouts and benefits upon his termination from

Valor. Also, he impersonated his physician, psychiatrist and a former employee to obtain disability insurance payments after his termination.

Jelen was caught before several schemes were completed and prior to succeeding with those termination crimes. His reward for all of this creative digital financial maneuvering was 70 months in prison and four years of supervised release, for bank fraud and attempted bank fraud. He was ordered to pay over $694,000 in restitution, as well. The judge cited greed and power as Jelen's motivations. No extra kudos were given for creativity nor his variety of efforts.

I'll wrap up this fraud category with a snapshot of what embezzlers currently use company credit cards to purchase, according AP Now, an accounts payable business intelligence firm.[49] The uses include:

- 77% for non-Amazon personal orders.

- 53% for personal Amazon orders.

- 22% for gift cards for personal use, included on expense reports.

- 17% for flights canceled with the funds not returned to the company.

- 15% for reimbursements from the company after the employee paid using card points.

You can tell by the nature of these thefts that, if they weren't large amounts, they could go unnoticed by anyone looking at the accounting books and not digging deeper into receipts or statements.

Pink-collar prevention tips:
- What is your company's policy on expense reports? Is it consistent for all employees? When administrative assistants see their bosses pad their expense reports it's hard to not want to enjoy some of the "good life."

- What is your policy on receipts? When I worked at one large firm, they raised the receipt requirement from $25 to $75. They decided the risk for their employees stealing was outweighed by the amount of time audit employees would have to review.

- Confused? Netflix[50] has an expense account policy that works if you only employ totally ethical, moral, honest, loyal, temptation-free and trustworthy people—good luck on that. The company's expense policy is five words long: "Act in Netflix's best interests." But you need to realize they have almost unlimited resources to be able to do this. As a small business owner I think it would be challenging in the human resources area to defend this policy when you are not consistent with all employees. Personally, I think having a good policy is better. There are plenty of resources online to assist you. You don't need to reinvent the wheel.

Chapter 4: Pink Flags

The world is full of obvious things which nobody by any chance ever observes.

— Arthur Conan Doyle

Do pink-collar crimes suddenly occur without warning? From my experience, I'd say that most of the time there are some warning signs of suspicious financial activities. I call them pink flags. These can be subtle. You must be looking for them, recognize what to look for and know where to look. But those flags do wave. The following are some crime scenarios and the common pink flags I've run across.

Time away from work

Consider the story of Burnice Geiger. She pilfered from her own father's bank in Iowa in the 1950s. Geiger stole $2.2 million, which is the equivalent of $17 million in today's dollars, by the time she was caught in 1961.[51] It took her 40 years to steal that much.

Besides causing her father's bank to have a run on it and shut down eventually, what made Geiger stand out? When she was arrested she was said to be "exhausted." Why? Because she admitted that she could never take vacations. This was back before Excel spreadsheets and Geiger had to be at work all the time to cover her tracks.

As co-author Stephen Dubner states in the book *Freakonomics*,[52] after Geiger's five year prison stint she went to work for a federal regulatory agency checking into people who didn't take vacations—the pink flag. You can't take a vacation if you're constantly hiding or altering financial statements and records.

More recently, I read a story in the *Sentinel Colorado* about Alyssa Costa, who was employed by a paving company in Aurora, Colorado.[53] She worked diligently to hide her fraud by making sure no one else had access to the company's payroll systems. At one point, she even cut short a vacation so she could come back and address the company's books. Her ill-gotten take? About $750,000 before being caught and sentenced to 15 years. Oh and this wasn't her first endeavor with fraud, as she had stolen close to the same amount from a previous employer likely using similar tactics. But the folks at the paving company had no way of knowing this criminal history.

I saw this tactic of assuming total control over company books at a dental practice case I worked on. We needed to know when the office manager was in the office working. She usually worked alone on Fridays. What happened on Fridays? That is the day the patients would come in and pay cash to get a better deal on their procedures. She would cut side deals with the patients. For example, if a patient owed $1,000 the office manager would propose that they pay $150 in cash for the next four Fridays so the bill would be taken care of. This was a case in which the office manager specifically targeted families that were non-banked (i.e. didn't have a bank account). The patients were primarily immigrant families that did not have dental insurance and paid with cash. She figured the patients would never go to law enforcement if they suspected anything. Why draw any attention to yourself from law enforcement? She had an advantageous position over them and siphoned off over $25,000 in cash.

The pink flag in this case? In six and a half years, the office manager had only taken one and one half days of vacation. During this time her husband had surgery for cancer. No time off. She was also in a car accident and came to work with a neck brace. She couldn't take time off because she needed to intercept the statements and answer the phone.

Sometimes patients would call and ask why their statement was incorrect. She would quickly say that it was just a mistake. The dentist also told me that the office manager fired three receptionists for "incompetence." Actually, I don't think that was the case. They were too good and too quick to answer the phone. She couldn't risk them answering the phones and having patients question their bills.

Another interesting tidbit about that case was the fact her son would show up at lunchtime for money. My kids have never shown up at my work for cash. Why did the son drop by during work for lunch and gas money? That's when she had lots of cash. She didn't have cash at night. She had that money from patient co-pays when she came to the office every day. Simple as that.

If I had an employee who had a family member showing up at work for money it might start to wave some pink flags for me. These can be little clues that just don't make sense and might make me curious.

The final clue in this case was when the office manager's car was repossessed in the office parking lot. Most everyone saw it. She was having financial issues and her co-workers knew she was struggling to make ends meet. But, I do remember the dentist telling me she was surprised that her office manager had a nicer washer and dryer than she had. Of course she did.

I've seen many cases where for whatever reason an employee was not able to get into work and that was when a theft was uncovered. An employee was unexpected hospitalized or became too ill to work. Maybe the employee got in a car accident. For whatever reason, this absence lead to an employer or colleague discovering an unknown bank account statement in the mail or get a call from a vendor or customer about a missing payment.

As you probably gather already, there is no shortage of stories about the discovery of pink-collar crimes associated with embezzlers taking many vacations as well as never taking them. For example, there's the case of

Rita Crundwell, the Queen of Pink Collar Crime—well-known in Dixon, Illinois just by her first name of Rita. She was even better known in the horse world. You see, Rita was on vacation when her $53.7 million embezzlement case was discovered, as noted in *Fraud Magazine*.[54] Unlike many employees who won't take a vacation for fear of getting caught, she actually took many vacations.

Rita was very comfortable in her job. After all, she started working as an intern for the City of Dixon when she was in high school. She was a career employee, a lifer. Rita had lots of vacation time to be able to go to Florida where her second home was located and enjoy showing horses. She was even so generous to the town that she would take unpaid leave.

But this one time her assistant, Kathe Swanson, needed to get the bank statements to do a reconciliation. Swanson called the bank and asked for all of the statements. *All* was the key word. They sent over all seven statements. But Swanson thought there were only six city bank accounts. The seventh account was Rita's fund for stolen money.

Here's one final story that's a twist on perpetrators rarely being out of the office for vacations or reasons like illness. A while back, I was interviewed for *North & South*, a magazine in New Zealand.[55]

"In the end, it was a dodgy belly that did her in. After embezzling $419,000 over seven years, Lynfield College accounts manager Rhonda Crabb was undone not by accountants or auditors, but by food poisoning. The day she phoned in sick, that Friday in November 2015, the task of preparing the banking for collection by a security company fell to her junior staffer. The woman, Crabb's junior, was the only other staffer in that small office, situated behind a service window that opened to the main reception foyer. By her reckoning, $2354.50 was missing. Rhonda Crabb didn't know it then, but she was already on her way to jail. No one suspected her until that day. Why would they? She'd been running the school's accounts for 19 years without incident."

Gambling it away

Casinos are built on customer losses not winnings. Show me a $50,000 a year employee who gambles regularly and I'll show you a financial disaster. I've seen it too often in my practice and the news. I consider gambling to be a major pink flag. According to the *2013 Marquet Report on Embezzlement*, approximately 24 percent of cases had gambling as a pressure.[56]

For example, the *Omaha World-Herald* reported that Annie Carbullido stole $1.2 million from the owners of a travel agency called Travel Faire, where she worked for 15 years.[57] The embezzlement was discovered while Carbullido was out of the office on a medical leave. She had cancer but still had the energy to go to casinos. She blew all of that money gambling.

From the *I can't make this up files*, "I was taking a break at work when I started playing the Queen of Diamonds game on my iPhone," said Nicol Evans. "When I saw the message pop-up on the screen that I had won $60,000 I took a screenshot just to make sure I was reading everything right," she told Michigan Lottery[58]. "When I ran into my boss' office he probably thought I was crazy, but when I showed him my phone he couldn't believe I had won either."

Evans was interviewed by the Michigan Lottery after winning $60,000. She said that she planned to use the money to pay off student debt, make extra Christmas purchases and possibly take a Disney cruise.

It turns out that Evans admitted stealing $328,000 from an addiction center she worked at. That's while she was receiving treatment for her gambling addiction. She was sentenced to five years of probation with a year on an electronic bracelet. The irony of this case is almost too much.

Gambling could be one of your lines in the sand when hiring. Of course there are plenty of people who can gamble recreationally, but in my experience I wouldn't take that chance. If I were to advise you about hiring employees, I might suggest that you casually ask about the local casino or Las Vegas to see their reaction. If they answered that they love going to the casino, that could be a deciding factor for your hiring decision. For me at least, it's a pink flag that's just too much to worry about.

Got a criminal record?

According to the *ACFE 2020 Report to the Nations*, approximately four percent of fraudsters have a criminal history.[59] This is down from five percent in the 2016 report. That may not seem like a lot but it's a 20 percent drop. Why is this number so small? In my experience, many embezzlers are terminated from their employment and not prosecuted when caught. The business may have any number of reasons for not contacting law enforcement. I always encourage the business to prosecute but I completely understand when they decide not to. Well, most of the time I understand.

One of the reasons businesses decide not to prosecute embezzlers might be the dreaded "skeleton in the closet." In one case I worked on, the embezzler named Carolyn, had a prior criminal record so she slipped through the cracks getting a new job after being convicted for theft. When she was caught the first time, Carolyn attempted to stop the business owner from contacting law enforcement. She told the business owner that she would contact the IRS and state tax authorities because Carolyn knew the owner was overly generous taking business expenses. "I know you are paying personal expenses out of the business," she said.

Luckily the owner called her bluff and contacted law enforcement. But now with a judgment for approximately $250,000, Carolyn needed another job to pay her restitution. And by the way, there was a gambling issue at the root of this mess.

What did Carolyn do when she was caught at a second business, a construction company? You guessed it, she made a threat. "I have told you before that I am being harassed by Bob [another employee] and there are inappropriate posters in the men's bathroom. I will contact the Bureau of Labor and Industries and file a complaint about harassment," she said to the owner. Luckily we knew her pattern, so the owner was forewarned and contacted the authorities.

I've conducted over 1,000 background investigations for federal and local governments and business owners. Out of all of the embezzlement cases I have investigated only two perpetrators had a criminal history.

But I do know that several employees stole money previously. How do I know this? If employees begin stealing within six months of starting a new position, it has been my experience they learned how to steal at a prior business. They may have been caught and kicked to the curb but not prosecuted.

Just because people don't have a criminal history doesn't mean they haven't stolen before. There is no national database of convictions. You must know where someone has worked and lived to perform a complete background check. And even background checks aren't foolproof.

Please don't make the mistake of thinking that when someone doesn't have a criminal record he or she has never committed a crime before. As Ronald Reagan said, "Trust but verify."

Life circumstances

All types of life circumstances can raise pink flags. For example, an addiction to prescription opiates led former CitiFinancial district manager Julie Phillips to embezzle close to $100,000 from the mortgage broker in 2009, according to a story in the *Boston Globe*.[60] That's what she told U.S. District Judge William Sessions as she wiped away tears during her sentencing hearing in Burlington, Vermont.

"Why did you do it?" Sessions asked Phillips. "You had a position of such authority that you had 33 employees working under you at eight institutions and a salary that put you upwards of $200,000 at one point." Phillips answered, "I don't have a good excuse, other than I let my addiction take over me." Sessions probed, "How did it start?" Phillips said she started using the pills following a surgery and things then veered out of control. "It just got worse," she said.

Phillips said that she stole the money for her own use or diverted it to other people of her choosing. Some of the money was then used to buy an undisclosed amount of oxycodone pills without a prescription, the U.S. attorney's sentencing memorandum said.

Phillips, who was indicted on a single bank fraud charge, did not contest the embezzlement charge and agreed to plead guilty to the charge. Sessions sentenced her to a year and a day in jail and ordered her to begin serving her prison term soon after sentencing. Her lawyer, Peter Langrock, had appealed to Sessions not to punish Phillips too harshly, saying Phillips addressed her addiction at a drug rehabilitation center and has a two-year-old daughter at home. Phillips' estranged husband, Andrew Phillips, had given custody of the child to her and he was said in court papers to be serving a jail sentence. So, he wasn't exactly available to care for the children if she were locked up.

Life circumstances and gender

I believe that many life circumstances and connected pink flags can be associated with female and male personality traits. Men feel they need to be the breadwinners. It's part of their masculinity to provide for their families. Women are the caregivers more often even though being the primary breadwinner is increasing.

A study related to this topic was conducted by Paul Klenowski with the results published in his book, *Gender, Identity, and Accounts: How White Collar Offenders Do Gender When Making Sense of Their Crimes*. The women

44

he researched "…claimed that the lack of capable males to support them necessitated that they assume the full responsibility as the family caregiver…"[61] For these women, the use of the defense of necessity was often coupled with fulfilling the caregiver role. They claimed that the necessity of their crimes was heightened because of their desire to protect or shield their family from harm. Women tended to emphasize their responsibilities as caregivers as the main driving force behind the necessity, coupled with the failures of others in their families—usually men.

Another part of the study I have seen up close and personal. Men often were "…merely seeking a justifiable reprisal for the wrong that had been committed against him." Whereas the men who used this technique pointed to generalized victims (e.g., the government), the women more often pointed to specific individuals who wronged them (e.g., employers).

As I continue to work on pink-collar crime and spread the word, many of these rationalizations and justifications come up during investigations. Knowing how men think and react in comparison to women is helpful when you're putting a case together and taking into consideration life circumstances.

Pink-collar prevention tips:

- A good embezzlement prevention and detection technique is to make sure that employees, especially office managers and those who handle the accounting take a minimum of one week vacation each year. Just taking a day or two off here and there can still allow an embezzler to cover up criminal activities. If they are away for a week at minimum, most businesses will have someone else do their work. That provides the opportunity for someone else to see past transactions, review current accounting activities, handle at least some customer or vendor transactions, or conduct an audit.

- If an employee's car is repossessed or he or she is subject to a judgment or lien, that's a likely indicator of having financial issues.

45

Not all employees who have financial issues will steal. But these are pink flags to be aware of and a reason to perform audits and other activities to ensure that all accounting and accounts are in order.

Chapter 5: Nonprofit & Governmental Fraud Cases

We make a living by what we get. We make a life by what we give.

—Winston Churchill

Many of us love to volunteer. We feel great helping out a good cause. Unfortunately, there's a dark side for some nonprofit operations—pink flags turn into egregious acts of fraud by everyone from employees to volunteers.

A while back, I spoke at a nonprofit that was connected with a municipality. I found out afterward that they realized some of the pink flags I had mentioned during my talk seemed familiar. They decided to take a deeper look at their finances. As a result, they found an embezzlement over several years by the office administrator.

The worst part of the story was that the attorney for the nonprofit opted not to press charges. The reason? It might be a credibility problem for the organization. The impact could be that donors wouldn't understand how the theft could have happened, questioned the organization's management and wondered how a potential thief could have been hired. With those doubts, maybe they wouldn't donate again.

The decision not to prosecute the perpetrator is disappointing. I understand how it might be bad public relations to announce it publicly. However, allowing someone to walk away from a theft is not a good outcome for many reasons. Employees see this happening and what do they think? Maybe if I steal and get caught, I'll only get a slap on the wrist or worse case I'll be fired. They might say to themselves, "Certainly since my employer didn't go to law enforcement in that case they won't go after me." This is one of the big reasons behind embezzlers become serial embezzlers. These criminals aren't held accountable for their actions. They just get kicked to the curb and move on to the next victim. The cycle is allowed to continue.

First, nonprofits have a responsibility to donors and potentially taxpayers to report fraud. I found it to be downright irresponsible of the attorney to stop their client from reporting that crime. Everything is about transparency these days. What's better, having the donors find out via the grapevine or being upfront with them about the changes that have been made so this won't happen in the future?

There's a term for this called Gresham's Law. It proposes that bad money—the theft of funds—will drive out the good money, which are the donations from the public or other entities. That's short-term thinking in my opinion.

I don't know if this was the case with a nonprofit called the Somerville Homeless Coalition. According to the story in the *Boston Globe*, a board member was reviewing the nonprofit's annual financial documents in 2015 and noticed something strange.[62] The financial report indicated that the chief operating officer earned $12,000 more than the nonprofit's top executive for the previous year.

More investigation revealed that the COO who handled the organization's finances had allegedly embezzled nearly $108,000 over a year and a half. This guy openly added the extra money directly to his paycheck, he used the organization's credit card for personal expenses and even included his middle-aged son in the group's health insurance. I don't know if the release of information about this crime ended up affecting the organization's bottom line. They'd probably never want to disclose that, but I do commend them on prosecuting this crime.

These stories bring to mind a motto often cited by nonprofits, "No money, no mission." I heard this from an accounting professor when she taught her course on fraud. If the money is gone, you can't fulfill the organization's mission. I don't know how many nonprofits have failed due to theft. If you look at businesses that close due to theft, then you could assume that nonprofits are similar. According to the *2020 ACFE's Report to the Nation*, the average business loses five percent of its revenue to fraud.[63] That's $50,000 for a $1 million budget, which could be a large chunk of a small nonprofit's entire budget. Fifty thousand dollars could pay for an employee.

The size of a nonprofit certainly is a factor with regard to the amount of the losses. Nonprofits have anywhere from very small budgets from small donations to large multi-million dollar budgets based on grants, large fundraising events and major gifts. Think Red Cross, Goodwill etc. as examples of larger nonprofits that likely would survive fairly substantial loss due to embezzlement.

And remember that fraud isn't limited to employees. It's not uncommon for volunteers to lack the proper training, skills and education to do the type of financial recording, reporting and auditing they're assigned to do. Plus, there's less segregation of duties if any at all in many small and even some larger nonprofits.

Consider small nonprofits completely run by volunteers. Have they taken courses in financial statement analysis, profit and loss statements? Most likely not. They volunteer because they're passionate about the mission of the nonprofit.

When I've been involved in nonprofits, rarely does anyone volunteer for the treasurer position. One reason might be that the job has too much responsibility and can be quite time-consuming. You have to go to the bank, go to the mailbox, sign checks, prepare reports, etc.

Ideally, nonprofits would try to appoint someone who's qualified to do the work. They'd double-check the treasurer's work, spot check the books regularly and even do a surprise audit now and then. Another good step would be to mail the bank statements to several board members for review. Of course it's important to ask if the board members know how to read a financial statement. There's really no excuse for not training people for such important positions. Many resources are available for nonprofits to learn about finances. There even are nonprofits that teach nonprofits about finances.

It's not difficult to find stories about volunteer treasurers committing fraud. Bonnie Brannock Davis was a longtime volunteer for the Giles County Lifesaving and Rescue Squad, according to *The Roanoke Times* article.[64] She had a good paying, $120,000 per year, job at The Chemical Lime Company in Ripplemead, Virginia until she was laid off. Eventually, she was convicted of stealing $65,000 from the Lifesaving and Rescue Squad and sentenced to two months in jail. Brannock Davis had no previous criminal history and had also volunteered for decades as a medic for Giles County Lifesaving and Rescue Squad. She did end up repaying the $65,000 to the nonprofit. Brannock Davis stated that she had already made anonymous donations to repay the organization over time.

What many embezzlers like Brannock Davis don't understand is that it's easier to steal money but much harder to replace the stolen funds. They may have intentions to repay but the mechanics of it are much more difficult. However, Brannock Davis actually did make two payments before her sentencing.

Interestingly, there was no extravagant spending on her part according to her attorney. I've seen this before. Volunteers may start stealing because of a pressure and it snowballs. Remember that they find the opportunity. In this case, Brannock Davis was a lifetime member of the nonprofit and had the job of handling the finances. Few people wake up in the morning and say they're going to steal. But at some point, something triggers this choice. In Brannock Davis' case, the loss of a good paying job most likely was the trigger. The lesson learned is to pay attention to your volunteers and their life situations. Consider negative events in their lives to be possible triggers for fraudulent acts.

In addition to volunteers and employees being liable for thefts, board members also have a fiduciary responsibility to organizations. If board members choose not to fulfill this responsibility they are opening themselves up to potential liability if a theft occurs. That liability could consist of civil and criminal charges. Does your nonprofit organization have what's called "directors and officers insurance?"

For example, board members of a Minnesota grain cooperative (a grain elevator business) were part of an insurance settlement tied to them overlooking the actions of Jerry Hennessey, the grain elevator's former manager. According to the story in the *Duluth News Tribune*, he stole $5.4 million which he used for a variety of lifestyle expenses.[65]

This case didn't end well for the Hennessey nor the board of directors. According to the newspaper article, "Defendants did nothing to supervise Mr. Hennessey, continuing to allow him—for at least 15 years—to defraud their elevator by writing checks for these [lifestyle] items and many others off the elevator checking account," Erik Ahlgren, the creditor's lawyer said. "Mr. Hennessey's scheme was there in plain sight, and the directors did nothing. Further, the directors never questioned inventory and other financial numbers that were cooked by Mr. Hennessey."

I worked a case for almost three years that was a dispute between the executive director of a non-profit and its board of directors. The upshot of that story was that everyone sued everyone and it ruined a community. Lives were changed and relationships forever altered. It was a sad case because the original mission was lost in all the drama. The only people who really came out unscathed were the attorneys. Because the executive director had purchased a directors and officers liability policy, their legal expenses were covered. If they didn't have the policy, the personal financial damage would have been catastrophic. Before you decide to join a nonprofit as an officer or director, you should check to see if they have one of these insurance policies.

Churches as embezzlement targets

One might think that churches are less likely to become the victims of embezzlement. After all, they only hire "good people," many of whom are church members. However, there are countless stories of churches being victimized by embezzlers. Sadly, not a week goes by when I don't see one form or another of embezzlement at a church.

Take the case of Sister Marie Thornton, aka Sister Susie. She was a nun who held a doctorate in education, served as an elementary school principal and was an assistant superintendent for the Archdiocese of Newark, New Jersey. According to a *New York Post* story, Sister Susie had a $180,000 a year salary working as a "trusted" financial officer. However, she was someone who couldn't cover the costs of her favorite pastime.[66]

Sister Susie's pastime was gambling—specifically, slot machines. She ventured to the Jersey Shore every weekend to visit her favorite casino and, of course, lost far more than she won. One weekend alone she lost $10,000. Over a 10 year period, she stole $850,000 from Iona College to fund her addiction. Sister Suzie's gambling money was easily acquired via a college business credit card. To cover her losses, the nun submitted false vendor invoices for reimbursement to the college. She also made the college cover her personal expenses.

Apparently, her addiction to gambling stemmed from a history of child abuse and a need for an "escape." Gambling made Sister Susie feel free from her past. Okay. That freedom didn't end well, because she was caught and sentenced to solitary confinement at her Philadelphia Sisters of St. Joseph convent for an undisclosed length of time as a compassionate alternative to prison. Unless you are working as a nun, you shouldn't consider this as a common punishment for the crime. Most likely you will do time behind bars.

There are endless examples of embezzlement, directly and indirectly connected with churches worldwide. According to the *2020 Status of Global Christianity Report* from the Center for the Study of Global Christianity, Christian organizations worldwide will lose $53 billion from financial fraud this year.[67] That's about 16 percent of the $320 billion in income they'll receive this year. Ecclesiastical crime is projected to reach $70 billion by 2025. These figures are categorized as amounts embezzled by "top custodians" of Christian monies.

Add to this the fact that about 80 percent of all cases of church fraud go unreported so they are not reflected in the international statistics.[68] This is according to Brotherhood Mutual, an insurance company specializing in serving churches. They found that only the big fraud cases, involving complex schemes and well-known individuals and organizations, are ever covered in the news. It's not surprising that, Brotherhood Mutual cites "…a recent survey conducted by a church fraud prevention organization found that nearly 60 percent of the churches surveyed had no way to report suspected financial crimes in their churches."

In wrapping up this topic, I want to recognize how nonprofits and churches provide many benefits to communities and I don't mean to paint them broadly as irresponsible or untrustworthy. Often they do work that no one else wants to do or has the resources to do. But there's a lot of money that runs through these organizations. Just because people believe in the mission, contribute their time and work many hours, doesn't mean those individuals would never steal.

It can be devastating for a nonprofit or church to suffer an embezzlement incident. Although many nonprofits can be well staffed, funded and managed, there are other smaller organizations that don't have those resources. Just because an organization is small please don't think it can't be a victim of embezzlement. Remember "No money, no mission."

Pink-collar prevention tips:

- Establish written financial policies that detail all procedures and requirements involving income and expenditures.

- Ensure that board members and/or employees who review financial activity have reasonable training to understand such matters.

- Conduct annual or semi-annual external audits by financial professionals if possible. Remember though that the number one way a fraud is detected is through tips by other volunteers and employees.

- Make it a policy to conduct background and credit checks on individuals with access to church accounts and money. Credit checks are great to see lifestyle and financial responsibility but many states have laws limiting the use of them. This is a dangerous area to dabble in because the Fair Credit Reporting Act has strict guidelines and penalties. Also, if you don't run the credit of a high level executive but you run the credit of lower level employees you are looking at a potential legal issue. Always check with your legal counsel about human resource and employment issues.

- Churches should arrange for at least two individuals to collect and count offerings made in cash. Then, deposit money at the bank as soon as possible and reconcile deposit slips with accounts after each bank deposit is made.

- Never allow a husband and wife—or multiple family members—to count cash together. It can be a good idea to mix up who counts together. Don't have the same two people counting weekly.

- Never establish a single individual to be responsible for all church financial matters. For example, one individual should never be tasked with counting donations, revenue from events and income from other sources.

- Always maintain adequate supervision of bank statements and reports involving financials by qualified individuals associated with the church or nonprofit.

Chapter 6: Corporate Fraud

Forgetting to include human nature in an equation can be devastating.

—Harry Markopolos, Bernie Madoff whistleblower

Did you know the movie *Psycho* had embezzlement as a theme? And another Alfred Hitchcock movie, "Marni," also had embezzlement as a theme. I wonder if this was because embezzlement usually is such a relatable personal type of crime, with temptation, secrecy, revenge, greed, relationships, risk and so many other compelling human characteristics at its core. Perhaps Hitchcock was a victim of embezzlement or he just knew people were fascinated by such crimes committed by "regular" people.

With all of the financial security and professional accounting staff that corporations have, how could theft be much of a problem? It is and it's no small problem. I've worked for large and small corporations and have seen plenty of fraud in both.

According to the ACFE *2020 Global Study on Occupational Fraud and Abuse*, the median loss for a business with under 100 employees was $150,000 per incident.[69] The median loss for a business with over 10,000 employees was $140,000 per incident. Depending on the fraudster's position, the losses vary widely. Higher level employees tend to steal more. Depending on the tenure of the fraudster, the losses also will vary. Potentially the employee has stolen over a much longer period of time, therefore the losses are larger.

Again, many people think that with large internal audit departments and external auditors checking the financial statements, employees would be crazy to try to steal from a company with all those resources. That's a faulty assumption. So much of the auditing function is only a sampling of expenses and revenues. And then if it's not "material," meaning not a big enough dollar amount of an item that would change any decisions drastically, they don't bother to dig deeper or report it. All of the large financial statement fraud cases, such as Foreign Corrupt Practices Act cases and other corporate malfeasance, have external auditors who didn't catch the frauds. Remember Enron and Arthur Anderson? Much like conducting a background investigation, you can't just check the "we have no fraud" box because you have auditors reviewing the financial reports and records.

Speaking of businesses that you'd think would have a tight grasp on financial matters, there's the classic corporate theft story of Minnie Mangum.[70] She kept the books at the Commonwealth Building & Loan Association in Port Norfolk, Virginia for nearly 30 years. Mangum was a Sunday school teacher and described as a pleasant person with a kind heart and a throng of admirers. But when caught at her thievery, she was arrested on charges of embezzling $3 million from the organization. This took place during a timespan from the 1920s to 1950s. That would be the approximate equivalent of $32 million in today's dollars.

Mangum was called a modern-day "Robin Hood" of the 20th century. She was reported to have given away $1.1 million over the years to 43 relatives and another $363,000 to 32 friends. She used stolen money to finance businesses for friends and relatives, to build them homes, and buy them a total of 85 automobiles. Days before her arrest, a Norfolk clergyman referred to Mangum as a "saint," according to a *Life* magazine profile about her. Friends circulated a petition in 1958 that urged the governor to free Mangum. They collected about 500 signatures, but on Nov. 21, 1959, Gov. J. Lindsey Almond denied the request.

A story not to go without a touch of humor, Mangum's name continued to be legend in Port Norfolk. She was memorialized at a restaurant called the Twisted Pig, where patrons could order "Miss Minnie's Perfect Burger." The menu item was inspired by this notorious resident, with the marketing phrase, "She didn't steal the full flavor of this awesome burger."

When I worked for a large corporation, we performed what were called *fraudits*. A fraudit was when I was brought in as the investigator because managers or executives thought something criminal may be going on. I would partner with corporate audit teams for their tools and expertise in the company's reporting and data functions. When the investigation resulted in a determination by audit staff and me that the individuals under suspicion were not committing a criminal act but merely making poor business decisions, the investigation became a fraudit.

That brings me to corporate expense reports, an area where pink flags often can pop up. Many corporations have specific guidelines for expense reports. The year I left employment at Nike, employees weren't asked to provide receipts for items less than $50. We were only required to state where we spent the money.

Of course, $50 seems insignificant to a large corporation, but it actually might become a larger issue if those small expenses added up over months or years for a lower level employee. Nike made a choice that it was not worth their time to monitor those receipts. But it's a slippery slope. All of a sudden, employees might realize that they could pad their expense reports with a few purchases—tax-free of course—that added up over the year. After all, employees could rationalize these expenses by thinking that the company owes it to them because they were away from home on business trips or the expenses were associated with their work. For example, having to pay dog sitters while employees are out of town might be a rationalization—in their minds, a reasonable excuse. The list of rationalizations is endless.

I can't tell you how many cases I've worked on in which thefts would start with some expense padding and then all of a sudden it expanded to other types of fraud. When people get away with one type of fraud they might get even more creative. They might add overtime, giving themselves raises and all sorts of other fraudulent activities.

Tone at the top

With all fraud, but especially fraud that takes place in a corporation, tone at the top with executives and managers is incredibly important. Watch out for unintentional precedents set by leaders. You can't expect the rank and file employees to behave honestly when they see higher ups getting away with company expensed luxuries and other so-called "perks."

Poor tone at the top can drive rationalization within the fraud triangle. What happens when lower level employees see the owner or the C-suite executive taking advantage of the business? It's often called "living out of the corporate checkbook." Employees are working long hours for a living wage. Yet, they see executives flying first class, having $10,000 dinners with "clients" at top restaurants and potentially committing other nefarious behaviors. But they don't see the executive getting in trouble for that behavior.

I often cite Warren Buffett, one of the world's greatest investors and richest men, when it comes to this issue. The following quote is from his *2018 Annual Letter:*[71]

> "Over the years, Charlie and I have seen all sorts of bad corporate behavior, both accounting and operational, induced by the desire of management to meet Wall Street expectations. What starts as an 'innocent' fudge in order to not disappoint 'the Street'—say, trade-loading at quarter-end, turning a blind eye to rising insurance losses, or drawing down a 'cookie-jar' reserve—can become the first step toward full-fledged fraud. Playing with the numbers 'just this once' may well be the CEO's intent; it's seldom the end result. And if it's okay for the boss to cheat a little, it's easy for subordinates to rationalize similar behavior."

Tone at the top, of course, is only part of the equation. While there's never an acceptable a reason for stealing, you need to understand the rationalization part of the fraud triangle. When you give your assistant your credit card bill or expense report that's filled with personal expenses, he or she can't help but see what you are doing. Or, the notice that you're cheating and stealing from the company or government. This can start a slippery slope for them to start their rationalization to steal. You're possibly chipping away at his or her set of values.

Another case of management setting precedents that result in financial consequences was with a woman named Susan Fowler and the ride share company Uber.[72] Fowler, an engineer at Uber, followed protocol and went to her human resources department due to concerns about a co-worker's inappropriate behavior. Fowler was told, "He was a high performer" and "...it was his first offense" so nothing would be done. Fowler was able to transfer to another group but she found out it was not that co-worker's first offense. Not even close to his first offense. It turned out that she took matters into her own hands with posts about it on Twitter. Due to that and other issues, Uber underwent many changes because of poor tone at the top. The loss of market capitalization due to the example set by leaders there was in the billions.

What employees don't realize is that if they start embezzling, they'll be held to a much different standard than the executives. At one place I worked, the company would prosecute lower level employees for expense account fraud but let higher level employees resign or even receive buyout packages when they were caught.

When employees are caught stealing and don't have the means to fight it they'll lose. When a company has higher level executives who steal, it just becomes embarrassing for the company. Management doesn't want to air their dirty laundry. So, it's swept under the rug. White- and pink-collar criminals experience two levels of "justice."

For example, take a look at the following graph published in *Report to the Nations' 2020 Global Study on Occupational Fraud and Abuse* by the ACFE the highlighting how organizations punish fraud perpetrators.[73]

How do victim organizations punish fraud perpetrators?

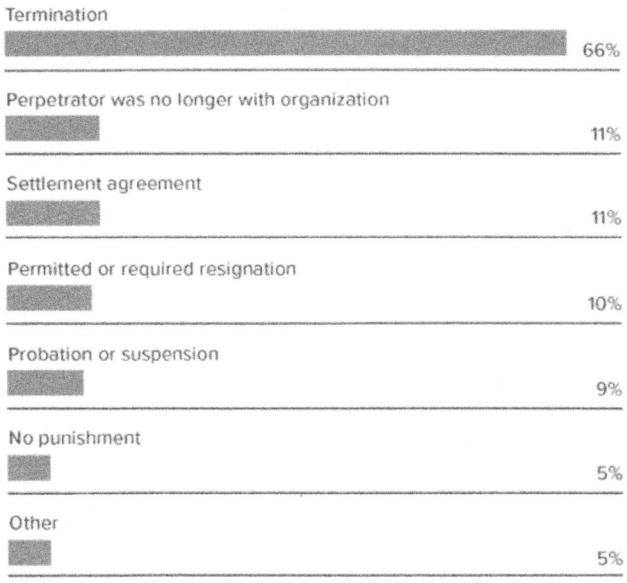

Termination — 66%

Perpetrator was no longer with organization — 11%

Settlement agreement — 11%

Permitted or required resignation — 10%

Probation or suspension — 9%

No punishment — 5%

Other — 5%

(Reprinted from Report to the Nations' 2020 Global Study on Occupational Fraud and Abuse)

This study found that 13 percent of owners or executives received no punishment for fraud, but only 2 percent of employees weren't punished. Also, 45 percent of owners or executives were terminated for fraud, but 76 percent of employees were terminated. And get this, only 59 percent of fraud cases were referred to law enforcement.

Another interesting graphic from the *ACFE 2018 Report to the Nations* showing punishment for fraud:[74]

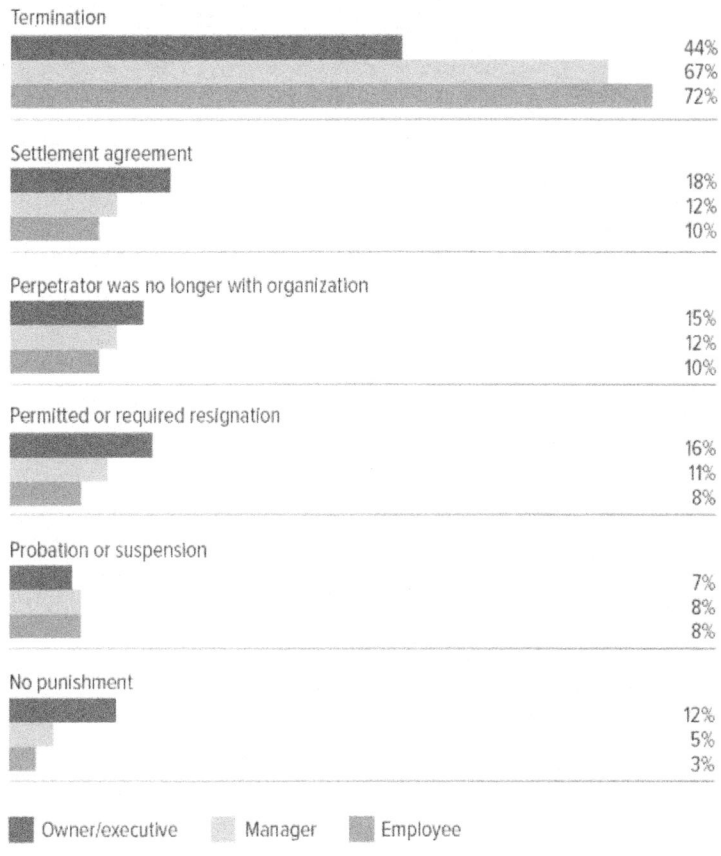

FIG. 42 **Does the perpetrator's position affect the punishment for fraud?**

Termination
44%
67%
72%

Settlement agreement
18%
12%
10%

Perpetrator was no longer with organization
15%
12%
10%

Permitted or required resignation
16%
11%
8%

Probation or suspension
7%
8%
8%

No punishment
12%
5%
3%

■ Owner/executive   ■ Manager   ■ Employee

Similar statistics are reflected in reporting rates for embezzlement. According to different reports and law enforcement agencies, only about 15 percent of embezzlement cases are referred to law enforcement. Why is that number so low? I have several thoughts about it. First, executives and managers are embarrassed by the thefts. They can't believe they didn't see the pink flags or the thefts. Second, if you think audits are bad to go through, try turning over your books—the real set—to law enforcement. That's scary. Law enforcement, depending upon state, local or federal level, has varying degrees of expertise. Smaller departments may have a detective who works embezzlement cases. A detective may or may not know a lot about deductions, tax law, etc. to properly evaluate accounting evidence. That can result in conclusions that go two ways, increased suspicions and further investigations or dismissal of possibly valid criminality due to lack of knowledge to spot it.

Reporting embezzlement can open quite a can of worms. For example, a medical clinic was the victim of an embezzlement scheme.[75] When the business owner confronted the suspect, she immediately threatened to report the owner to the IRS. The suspect told the owner that she knew various personal expenses were being written off to the business. The owner stood firm and didn't back down.

Many owners might not go to law enforcement in a situation like that. Instead they may just kick the suspect to the curb. However in this case, the perpetrator was convicted and given a minimal sentence. After all it was her first offense, we thought.

Next, this embezzler went to work at a small business. That's where I came in. When it was time to fire her for stealing $250,000, I told the detective to warn the owner that she would to try to stop the prosecution. The detective asked me how I knew this. I explained that I had tracked down the previous investigator to find out about the prior embezzlement and that's when I was told about the suspect's threats to go to the IRS.

Sure enough, when the owner confronted the embezzler she immediately said she had warned him about inappropriate sexual behavior by employees and she was going to turn him into the Bureau of Labor and Industries. But he knew this was coming and was prepared to call her bluff. It worked. She never contacted the agency.

Even if an employer is innocent of these charges, it still costs quite a bit to defend yourself against such charges. Many employers will back down. This is what I call the "Get out of jail free card." Employees, especially ones who are stealing, are fully aware of what's going on in a business. They're often the right hand person of the owner. They know the secrets.

That said, you don't want to be put in a position like this. Don't give anyone the option of a threat against you. But if you're concerned about this type of situation, you need good legal counsel to protect yourself.

Small Business

Large corporate fraud has its own potential repercussions. However, fraud can cause many small businesses to lay off employees, freeze wages, sell assets or even go out of business. They just can't stand to lose thousands of dollars or more. And the emotional toll of being deceived by a trusted employee can be devastating to the owners and the future of the business. According to the Better Business Bureau, approximately 30 percent of all business failures are due to embezzlement.[76] Nearly one-third!

Here's an example of this. The *Missoulian* reported an embezzlement case about Eureka woman named Roseann Robyn Kipp who was the office manager for the Eureka Economic Development Office.[77] She stole approximately $50,000. The scale of the embezzlement, according to Assistant U.S. District Attorney Ryan Weldon, had caused the office to close. Maybe it was a budget killer or perhaps the office was shut down because the manager was blamed for not preventing the crime.

Another story I ran across was about a family-owned electrical company. Two brothers owned the business. They each had their own responsibilities. What happened when a pink-collar criminal devastated the business? The brothers blamed each other. They questioned each other about why each didn't catch it. Both thought it was the other's responsibility. They figured that if the other had been paying better attention the theft never would have happened. This was no way to end a 50 plus year business, but it did. Sadly, money could be replaced but the relationship was forever altered.

One victim of this small business embezzlement said in a podcast, "I managed the business out of the bank account instead of managing the processes she [the embezzler] was using." He went on to say, "I'm not really big enough to have any processes and that leaves the door wide open."

While you may not think you're not big enough to suffer from embezzlement, the perpetrator might be perfectly happy only to steal $5,000. Many businesses can easily afford that, but many can't.

Pink-collar prevention tips:

- The most important piece of advice I can give to small businesses about preventing fraud is always to have a healthy dose of skepticism. Go with your gut. It's usually right. However, never rush to judgment. If you suspect something, start listening closely to all of your employees, including the suspect. Does the salary match the lifestyle? Has the employee changed his or her behavior recently?

- Review your business' or organization's credit reports on a regular basis. Maybe there's an account you aren't familiar with, missed payments or other indications that recorded financial activities aren't accurate. A common fraud scheme is for an embezzler to open accounts under the business' name or even the owner's name and use it to siphon off money.

- Good fraudsters know when auditors are coming to review their accounting books. Be sure to mix up those dates. Regularly conduct surprise audits on petty cash. Also, use occasional surprise audits on new vendors. For example, Gary Foster, a Citigroup VP, said that he was able to pull off his $22 million embezzlement by keeping the numbers relatively small.[78] He also stole money in the middle of the month instead of the end dates when auditors might be more alert to discrepancies. Frequent surprise audits likely would have caught these thefts early on.

- If you have a secure building site, be sure everyone uses his or her own entry code or cardkey. This is very important in cases when employees' access to records can be used to show dates and times they were in the office as illegal activities were taking place. This means no one should ever share codes or cardkeys.

- Periodically, conduct a "snapshot" of your accounts. Check with an employee who handles the books to ask about a specific transaction or two—maybe a vendor payment or bank transaction. This is a way to let that employee know that you are checking your accounts online. If an employee says something that sounds suspicious, is evasive when asked questions or an answer doesn't ring true, further investigation is called for.

Chapter 7: Healthcare

There is not a crime, there is not a dodge, there is not a trick, there is not a swindle, there is not a vice which does not live by secrecy.

—Joseph Pulitzer

Embezzlement in medical offices is a huge problem. The Medical Group Management Association found that nearly "83% of 688 practice managers were at some point affiliated with medical offices where employee theft occurred."[79] About 18 percent of these incidents involved thefts of $100,000 or more, stolen in small amounts by the most trusted employees.

Do you know that nearly 49 percent of dental practices experience employee theft?[80] And, according to the American Dental Association's Council on Dental Practice, around 46 percent of practices experience employee theft more than once. Another study shows as many as three out of five dental practices are embezzled. I've seen plenty of these cases in my work. As with other embezzlement cases, there are common vulnerabilities, pink flags and preventive actions. Let's take a look at some stories about dental and other medical practices.

Dental Office Theft

Maybe the best way to start a discussion about dental office theft is by addressing why dental practices are so hard hit by embezzlement. First, these practices are generally smaller than most medical practices.

Secondly, there's not much segregation of duties among employees due to the office size. Thirdly, dental practices often have a considerable amount of cash running through them due to cash co-pays, out-of-pocket expenses and payments from uninsured patients. And, even though the many purchases of supplies from various vendors rarely are made using cash, those transactions add up quickly and represent a vulnerability related to cash-flow.

The fact is that many dentists have no idea how much cash and other financial transactions are running through their practices during any given month. Although we don't hire dentists based on their profit and loss statements, we certainly don't want our dentists to be distracted by employee theft.

Many dental practices hire CPAs to prepare financial statements and prepare tax returns. Some CPAs even take care of payroll. So, I've had dentists ask me why their CPAs didn't catch the fraudulent activity? Unfortunately, few CPAs actually look for fraud. It's not in their engagement letter with the client.

I have to explain that employees who steal are in the weeds, so to speak. They often know what the accountants are looking at and what they are looking for when examining the books or other accounting materials. I can't tell you how many times I've talked with pink-collar criminals and learned that they know exactly where to hide their expenses or thefts. If you happen to be a dentist reading this section you should take a look at Prosperident's Hall of Shame.[81] They profile individuals who have stolen from dentists. Maybe you'll want to look through the perpetrators and see if one of your employees is listed.

At least one of my cases is included in the Hall of Shame. I worked this case while at the sheriff's office. The story began with a dentist's wife receiving a call from the bank used by their practice. Fortunately, the bank called their home number rather than the office. The bank representative asked if there was a reason why one of the insurance checks should be deposited in an employee's account. That's when their employee's embezzlement scheme started to unravel.

Elizabeth Eisert was the office manager in this embezzlement case.[82] She was the right hand employee for the dentist and was always there to control access to the dentist. Eisert had all the answers whenever the dentist questioned her about the business. Although, he just wanted to do his work so he never thought twice about her answers to his inquiries. The dentist trusted her and she made his practice run smoothly. As is common with these types of cases, Eisert had a close relationship with the dentist and his family, even attending family events. This is a textbook example of how there tends to be a heightened level of trust when a business relationship extends into a personal one.

When I talked with one of the hygienists after the theft, I learned that office life there was a different story for the hygienists. Eisert was controlling. She was moody and when staff questioned her at the wrong time, they would pay for it with verbal abuse.

Over the years, the hygienists didn't receive raises due to Eisert's theft. The dentist was generous but there was only so much he could do when his practice was being embezzled to the tune of approximately $100,000 per year. Whenever the dentist asked Eisert why they were having cash flow issues, he also would mention the fact that he did a few more root canals or other high-ticket procedures that month so revenue should be higher. She would come up with strategic responses along the lines of, "Remember, we had the lease payment on the equipment" or an expense that he had forgotten they had incurred in the practice.

It went on like that for years. He ended up taking out loans occasionally. Another factor in the way of him questioning Eisert further was that his wife watched over the books. But like with many businesses that have family members involved, she was busy raising the kids and also trusted Eisert.

This theft was the hardest thing the dentist and his wife had gone through as partners. She initially thought it must be a mistake when the bank called her at home with that question about the deposit. If they had called the office, Eisert might have been able to cover up the theft and could still be stealing from the practice.

Eisert ended up stealing over $1 million from her employer. She had numerous issues going on in her life. Her husband had lost his middle class job, she had a sick mother-in-law, grandkids had expensive hobbies, plus she had a gambling addiction. When I reviewed her bank statements I saw almost daily charges on her account. There was no business listed, only an address. I did an internet search for the address and found it to be a video poker establishment.

Life was not so great at home. She took solace daily at lunch by eating her bologna sandwich while stuffing the video poker machine with stolen money. I recently Googled Eisert and saw her obituary. She did her time in prison, but I'm certain this chain of events didn't help her physical and mental health. This is not the first time I have seen a pink-collar criminal die either while in prison or shortly after. Remember Minnie Mangum? She died two years after completing her prison sentence.

In addition to theft of money in dental practices, I've seen materials such as whitening treatments being stolen. Also, most dentists provide free or very reduced cost care for their employees and their families. But some employees even take advantage of that generosity by committing insurance fraud. They bill insurance for the procedures and then get the reimbursement. This can really cause problems for a dentist depending on the state and their insurance fraud laws.

Additionally, dentists prescribe medications and that can be abused. I know a CPA whose dentist brother had his prescription pad stolen. You don't want the Drug Enforcement Administration knocking on your door to investigate prescription fraud.

This reminds me of case I read about in the Ventura County *Citizens Journal* was about Kristina Vargas, a fraudster who worked in a dental office.[83] She fraudulently used a dentist's information to obtain the pain killer Carisoprodol on 11 separate occasions. The local Pharmaceutical Crimes Unit detectives collected evidence and conducted interviews to confirm the fraudulent prescriptions. Vargas was arrested shortly after that. This incident being reported in the newspaper certainly wasn't positive for the dental office's reputation.

Other medical office theft

Let me start this section about embezzlement in other medical offices with a case in which I interviewed the perpetrator. Lisa Marie Sundquist saw an investigative report on the local TV news station that flashed her mugshot on-screen.[84] Her friends started calling to tell her that they saw the broadcast. That's when Lisa reached out to me and we met for coffee. I recall that our chat must have gone on for almost two hours. By the way, being able to listen to a pink-collar criminal tell his or her story is very interesting. It's fascinating to hear their side of the story.

Lisa was smart, attractive and hard working. She went to work for a small surgical practice with six surgeons. Two of the surgeons were toward the end of their careers. Two others were mid-career. And another two were just starting out. This created a certain dynamic within the practice. Each of the three groups had different goals for their careers and finances.

When Lisa started her new job at the practice, they were still using paper and pencil to schedule patients. The practice's administrators were sisters who had never had any type of office management or bookkeeping training. Lisa quickly saw that the practice was not billing secondary insurance. She estimated the practice had lost over $1 million due to this oversight. The bills were not able to be resubmitted due to strict deadlines imposed by the insurance companies. Due to the urgent need, Lisa got right to work upgrading and updating the entire business management of the practice. She was computer and tech savvy so she started billing correctly. She updated the practice's software to a new program that would be much more efficient. The doctors were happy with the improvements, plus they were making more money.

I asked Lisa to tell me about the first time she stole money from the practice. She said that one Friday the practice received a check for approximately $8,000. The bill wasn't accounted for in either system. She said she went to the bank and requested the $8,000 check be made to a cashier's check. She kept the check over the weekend. That's how it started. After the initial theft, the scope of her crime expanded as she started writing checks to herself. She coded them in the software program to various cost centers such as printing, supplies, etc.

I'm compelled to add an observation and piece of advice related to this case with Lisa. Many times, doctors don't see the need for additional training for administrative employees. They think of the job as just accounts receivable, accounts payable and customer service with patients. This is a mistake. Doctors need to understand how training for administrative employees is absolutely necessary to maintain a viable practice.

This case with Lisa also exemplifies how there usually is a tipping point for embezzlement. Think of your first kiss or your first boyfriend or girlfriend. Your memories are much more vivid right away than months later. Dr. Linda Grounds, a forensic psychologist in Portland, Oregon, told me to always ask about the first time a suspect stole when I interview them. It's a significant moment in their lives and is a memorable marker for them.

Every Friday the senior surgeon at this practice would meet with the office's CPA. They would pull up the accounting software report. Never once did they actually pull a check to see if it matched the entry in the bookkeeping system. That's how Lisa got away with stealing approximately $250,000. Can you imagine sitting in the office every Friday and wondering if they were going to look at a check and you'd be caught? The stress was unimaginable at first but eventually Lisa realized they never even bothered to look at checks.

It turned out that she used the money for cosmetic surgeries, tanning salons, restaurants, clothes and other luxuries. It wasn't like she was living a visibly extravagant life, although the breast implants and tummy tucks weren't reflective of a totally conservative lifestyle.

Lisa ended up quitting the practice before she was found out. She said she always knew someday the doctors would figure out she had stolen from them. Eventually, she received a call from a local detective. Lisa was asked if she knew why he was calling and she said that she did. It took several more weeks for the detective to get back to her. They set up a time for an interview. Lisa became physically sick at the interview. She walked into the room and saw the detective had binders of financial documents. The practice's CPA had discovered the crime and provided documentation to the police.

Lisa tried to make a deal financially with the practice. Her family was able to come up with approximately $50,000 to gain some leniency. The practice declined. Lisa was sentenced to 57 months. The embezzlement devastated the practice. Several of the doctors left the group. I doubt they ever recouped the entire amount of restitution. Last I knew, Lisa was waitressing. I don't know many waitresses who can save an additional $200,000 plus interest.

Medical practices vary in size and revenue but they all have billing systems that are not 100 percent embezzlement proof. Do you want your doctor to spend time learning about billing and administrative tasks or spending time learning about medicine and caring for you? Most doctors' skill sets are better suited to medicine than profit and loss. This is how and why medical embezzlement occurs so often in practices, especially small ones.

Pink-collar prevention tips:

- Train more than one person on the bookkeeping system and rotate people through the various processes. This way, your employees can check each other's work for mistakes and anomalies. Cross-training employees helps to create a transparent financial environment. This also reduces opportunities for theft by ensuring that no one person wields too much power over the accounting system.

- Regularly receive and review financial statements. Set aside time with your office manager or accountant to understand line items and transactions. Check past reports to see how the numbers align. Be sure to ask questions if you see a line item growing or inconsistencies in revenue or expenses.

- Develop a budget to structure your financial affairs. This can really help you detect fraud. Compare your productivity reports with the income statements. Do your cash receipts match current and recent productivity reports? Do your expenses align with the productivity reports? When cash that's coming into your practice isn't in line with your budgeted forecast model, that's a pink flag waving. A pink flag also should appear if expenses are above the forecast model.

- When you examine your income statement, using a cash-basis accounting system, you'll see the cash that was received and recorded. But the expenses associated with the revenue generating activity may have been paid over a longer time. You need to be aware of this uncoupled effect between income and expenses. This can make it easier for someone to slip in phony expenses or skim revenue off the top.

- It's always a good idea to do a thorough background check on all of your employees, especially those who handle your money. This check should cover criminal and financial records. Be sure to consult your legal counsel regarding the financial and credit checks. Many states have strict rules regarding credit checks. And even though this is a wise policy, remember that background checks may not reveal previous unprosecuted crimes.

PART THREE

Getting Past the Theft

Chapter 8: And Justice For... Some

It's that every now and again—not often, but occasionally—you get to be a part of justice being done. That really is quite a thrill when that happens.

—Andrew Beckett, character in the film *Philadelphia*

You did everything right when you discovered the crime that had taken place in your office or organization and that chapter of life is closed. Yet, something doesn't seem right—the experience didn't make you feel whole. You don't feel justice was served. And to pour salt on the wound, it cost you time and money. Unfortunately, this is how the story often ends with embezzlement. When cases are closed, most victims feel unfulfilled about how justice was served and their experience with the criminal justice system. It's just not something many victims talk about.

This is one of the hardest parts of my job, telling victims that the system grinds slowly and it may not seem like it even works. First time offenders, like many are, may just get a slap on the wrist. Often they'll only get probation. While the U.S. is a very litigious country, the criminal justice system is incredibly overburdened. Just getting a case to grand jury can take months.

In one case, I had the victim turn over all of the records and documents only to have it take almost a full year to get the accused criminal indicted. The victim was an accountant and the books were clean. She did all the work. But, law enforcement agencies don't just take a victim's word for it in cases like these. They must show the money trail.

And because this case was incredibly well documented, the suspect was indicted. However, with continuances and court dates being backlogged it took another year for the legal resolution. Meanwhile, the victim had to pay her attorney thousands of dollars to monitor the case and attempt to work out a resolution that was acceptable.

How many businesses can afford to pay their own attorney after being embezzled? And that doesn't even account for the fact that the victims really don't understand why it's in their best interests to have an attorney do this. Remember, you need to get back to work to recover from the stolen funds, plus you have all of the legal costs.

The sad truth is that most pink-collar criminals never go to trial. That's even though the evidence is generally clear cut and they don't have a defense. The perpetrators likely have spent the money and don't have funds for a good attorney. They may be able to get a public defender but public defenders are overworked too, so their defense might not be all that strong. You might ask: What if the victims say the suspects confessed? They wrote it down and signed it. Well, this isn't "CSI Embezzlement." Cases are more complicated than that and they take much more time to prosecute. It's not like with TV or movies when everything is resolved within the episode's length.

Also, remember that most cops don't become cops to examine spreadsheets associated with financial crimes. There are countless notebooks and data to plow through. The cases are drawn out and can be messy depending on the business' bank records. Some cops who are assigned to fraud units even see financial crimes as a burden. Show me a cop who likes data and notebooks more than going to the shooting range, dealing with emergency situations and driving fast cars and I'll show you an IRS agent.

That said, local police, sheriff's offices or a federal agencies likely will devote more urgent attention to red-collar crimes. You may recall that those are financial crimes that end up with violence.

A horrific example of a red-collar crime was a case about a law firm in Florida. Linda Renae Williams was an accountant at a firm.[85] One day, she was confronted about irregularities in the firm's finances and left work abruptly. The next day, Williams got up early and drove her car to the road her supervisor's home. Allegedly, she rammed her supervisor's car head on, then left the scene of the accident. Both women showed up at the law firm's office about an hour later. When they met, Williams stabbed her supervisor with a five-inch filet knife. The supervisor was taken to the hospital for stitches and survived. Williams was jailed with her bail set at $1 million. The case has not yet been resolved as of the time of this book.

Another recent red-collar crime case allegedly took place in Idaho. Lori Isenberg is awaiting trial for the murder of her husband.[86] She previously plead guilty to embezzling $570,000 from the North Idaho Housing Coalition. The day her husband's body was found was when she was arrested for the theft. She said he had a medical episode of some type and fell overboard while they were out boating. The coroner later determined he had a lethal amount of Benadryl in his system. The case has so many twists and turns. It's hard to believe one person could do so much damage.

All of these cases lead me to a question you might be asking: What's the difference between going to the local police or sheriff's office and going to a federal agency? I hate to say it but it depends. Local law enforcement typically deals with thefts of lower dollar amounts on average. Once in a while, a case involving a small dollar amount may have an angle that a federal agency is interested in though. You may even need to have your lawyer "sell" the case to a law enforcement agency that could more actively investigate or prosecute a case.

Prosecutors at any level in the justice system want cases they can win. They aren't going to take a weak case because they're held to certain standards too. While many people think the justice system is fair, it also must be run as efficiently as possible. Prosecuting a case takes a huge amount of time and money. That's one reason why only around four percent of all federal cases go to trial. It depends on the jurisdiction but the percentage is low. Most defendants take a plea deal, anyway. That benefits them within the federal system and they're rewarded for cooperating.

In other words, defendants must be really sure they can win against the prosecutor's case. They'll surely be penalized if they lose. In these cases, the evidence is generally very clear cut too. That's why a plea deal— seeming fair or unfair—makes sense for the criminals and justice system. And what about the victim here and justice being served? Again, that's a tough call. It depends on the victim's expectations and the realities of our justice system.

The Inner Workings of Cases

When I do criminal defense work—versus prosecution—it's my job to be objective and look at all the evidence. As Certified Fraud Examiners, we have a code of ethics which doesn't allow us to say someone is innocent or guilty.[87] That's up to the courts to decide. We just give the facts.

If the evidence points to theft, it's my duty to inform the attorney. We look for ways to mitigate the circumstances from that point on while working on a plea agreement. I'd never tell a defendant to go to trial if there were any evidence that showed theft.

When I'm working with the victim of a theft, we'll attempt to find evidence of any assets that can contribute to restitution for the victim. Maybe a relative of the perpetrator will reimburse a large part of the amount stolen. Perhaps the perpetrator has a retirement fund that can be cashed out. It could be helpful to look at where the money went to see if there are any assets that were purchased with stolen funds that could be worth something if liquidated.

However in my experience, people who embezzle generally spend the money on their lifestyle. No one steals to save for future expenses and rarely for retirement. They most often buy cars, property or jewelry. Those assets might be worth something to fund at least some restitution.

In one pink-collar case I worked on, the criminal offered about 20 percent of what she stole as a one-time restitution payment. Her family got the money together. Paying the victim would not have kept her out of prison but may have lessened the length of her sentence. However, the victims were so angry they turned down the offer. The court then ordered her to pay restitution in the amount of $250,000. She went to prison. Upon release, she wasn't been able to find a well-paying job in her field so she worked as a waitress. The victims will never come close to getting that $50,000 in restitution they were offered—perhaps penny wise and pound foolish. Again, this is when you need a good attorney and team to guide you to make the best decision for you in the long run.

In another one of my cases, a dentist's office manager stole $1 million over 10 years. Much of it was spent on gambling, but she did have a motor home and, surprisingly, actually made contributions to a small retirement account. She sold the motor home and cashed out the retirement account as part of her restitution.

This brings to mind the value of interviewing an embezzler's co-workers. They may know what the suspect has bought with stolen money and something about his or her lifestyle. Just remember that you never should take the suspect's word for where the money went.

Also, many victims may want to know if the suspect's spouse was involved in the crime. On the flip side, I've had cases in which the significant other wondered about the couple's new and improved lifestyle. Spouses certainly have been known to not want to know what's going on to rationalize the opportunity to enjoy an upgraded lifestyle. For example, Bernie Madoff's wife, Ruth, claimed to be unaware of his financial scam. In any case, it's always worthwhile to find out if the perpetrator's spouse has assets that can be seized.

Another case I worked was one in which a grand jury wanted to indict the significant other of the suspect. The man was even subpoenaed before the grand jury. I didn't get to listen to the grand jury proceedings, but apparently he was quite uncooperative discussing his girlfriend's $450,000 theft from which he benefited by enjoying their lifestyle. He was not going to admit he had any knowledge of the thefts.

Both the detective and I told the assistant district attorney that based on all the bank records there was no way we could prove beyond a reasonable doubt any money had been directly given to him. We think he just buried his head in the sand and didn't want to know how they afforded to shop and go out to eat all the time. That said, I don't think he waited for her while she was in prison.

Once in a while you'll see a case in which the spouse also is indicted. It's not typical, but I do know prosecutors will use the threat of indicting co-conspirators to get leverage over the suspect.

If you're reading this book because your spouse has been caught embezzling or you think something financially may be off, you might find it interesting to read a *Forbes* column by Walt Pavlo titled, "White Collar Wives."[88] It includes some valuable background and advice.

The Sad Truth

As I mentioned previously, only about 15 percent of all embezzlement cases are taken to law enforcement. Can you imagine if every victim of theft were to report these crimes to law enforcement? The courts probably would be overwhelmed, with cases backed up for years. Our criminal justice system is not designed for speed. Even now, both victims and suspects can't understand why it takes so long to complete the process. Some people would be surprised to know that suspects often just want to get it over with too due to the threat of prolonged prosecutions. People on both sides of the crime just want to move forward with their lives.

Most likely at the end of the legal process, no one will be fully satisfied. Much like with an unamicable divorce, no one is a winner. The victim is not going to receive full restitution anytime soon, if ever. The suspect may go to jail or prison. And then upon release, the convicted individual will have a difficult time reintegrating back into society with a criminal record. Any skills he or she had, such as accounting, likely won't be part of a future job.

I would love to say that all's well that ends well, but I haven't found that to happen very often. It's just an unfortunate part of being a victim in that you really won't feel good at the end. And justice may or may not really be served.

Pink-collar prevention tips:
- Try to make decisions regarding prosecution and restitution pragmatically rather than being driven mostly by emotion. Trusted advisors can be very helpful in guiding you to make decisions in your best interests.

- Weigh consideration of restitution for stolen funds against the odds that it actually can/will be paid by the perpetrator. Sometimes obtaining partial restitution up-front may be prudent versus gambling on receiving more money over time.

- Understand that the criminal justice system is not quick and embezzlement cases may not lead to prosecution or truly satisfying results. Do everything you can to support your case but know your limits for legal expenses and time to devote to this process.

- If your spouse may be an embezzler, look into potential civil penalties, unpaid tax on stolen funds, and of course the many other legal ramifications for you and your family.

Chapter 9: Justifications for Crimes

The trust of the innocent is the liar's most useful tool.

—Stephen King

I read as much as I can about women and crime. It's so interesting to understand the emotional and intellectual processes that take place when women (and men) confront a decision point about whether or not to commit a crime. Also, I'm fascinated by the psychology of repeated acts of embezzlement.

To that end, I recently came across the term *neutralization*. The concept was introduced by David Matza and Gresham Sykes as they studied the psychological aspects of juvenile delinquency. The definition of neutralization from Wikipedia is as follows: "Techniques of neutralization are a theoretical series of methods by which those who commit illegitimate acts temporarily neutralize certain values within themselves which would normally prohibit them from carrying out such acts, such as morality, obligation to abide by the law, and so on. In simpler terms, it is a psychological method for people to turn off 'inner protests' when they do or are about to do something they themselves perceive as wrong."[89]

Now, think about embezzlers and how they usually find ways to rationalize their criminal acts, even celebrate them in some cases. Matza and Sykes came to believe that delinquents justified their illegitimate actions by using the following five methods of neutralization:

1. The denial of responsibility.

2. The denial of injury.

3. The denial of the victim.

4. The condemnation of the condemners.

5. The appeal to higher loyalties.

Although the technical term neutralization was new to me, I've experienced it every time I've interviewed suspects about their involvement in a crime. Many investigators know that it's helpful to understand neutralization to get the story or the confession from suspects. This also is a way to come to terms with the age old question most of us ask when trying to wrap our heads around crimes: "What were you *thinking* when you did that crazy thing?"

Now I know that understanding some of the psychology of crime, such as with neutralization, doesn't necessarily help you prevent embezzlement or resolve it after it occurs. But, this bit of knowledge may help you comprehend the thinking behind the criminal's acts.

Another aspect of neutralization that's even more fascinating is the difference between men and women and their use of neutralization. There's a very interesting paper that features a study with 40 subjects, split with 20 males and 20 females. The title is, "Gender, Identity, and Accounts: How White Collar Offenders Do Gender When Making Sense of Their Crimes" by Paul M. Klenowski, Heith Copes and Christopher W. Mullin, published in *Justice Quarterly*.[90]

As I mentioned in a previous chapter, the researchers' interviews made it clear that all male and female subjects used different neutralizations to justify their crimes. However, their justifications varied by gender in many cases. The women claimed that the main driving forces behind the necessity for their crimes were their desires to protect or shield their families from harm as well as their responsibilities as caregivers. For men, they sought "…justifiable reprisal for the wrong that had been committed against him."

If you're a business owner who has experienced employee embezzlement, I think you'll relate to this. And knowing how men think and react in comparison to women is helpful when you and I are trying to put a case together. Business owners don't intentionally hire criminals. But individuals' situations change and they may consider stealing as the only way they can get out of a bad situation.

By the way, a colleague of mine in criminal justice saw a Twitter tweet I posted about someone stating he or she made a "mistake" and started stealing. My colleague reached out to me and told me in parole and probation they don't use that term. They make it clear it was a <u>choice</u> to commit the crime. Referring to crimes as mistakes tends to diminish the criminals' personal responsibility for their actions. But we should remember that people who make bad choices are still human. To investigate these crimes fully, we must maintain some empathy to learn more of the story from suspects.

Optimism Bias

Related to justifications for pink-collar crimes is the justification for bias by victims. Optimism bias is a cognitive bias that causes some people to believe that they're less likely to experience a negative event. Maybe that should be a showcase trait of those who don't believe they could be victims of fraud.

Maybe they think they're too smart. Perhaps they're convinced that they only hire "good" people. Or, they know they have an experienced CPA watching out for them.

What's even more frightening is that some people have even higher rates of optimism bias toward negative events. This is called the valence effect. It means these people have unrealistic optimism that's greater for negative events than positive ones.

In my presentations, especially to small businesses, participants never talk about how fraud could happen to them. They believe that fraud can happen to the business owners sitting next to them, but not to them. But to be capable of spotting criminal actions by employees, you must come to terms with the fact that you indeed could be a victim.

Pink-collar prevention tips:

- Don't assume that the perpetrator of an embezzlement crime will face the reality of the crime. In other words, the embezzler likely won't be thinking rationally or honestly because he or she may deeply believe the rationalizations used during the period of the crime.

- I certainly don't want you to live in constant fear about becoming a victim of embezzlement. On the other hand, I do want you to accept the reality that it can happen to you and take ongoing precautions to prevent or at least minimize the chance that you'll be a victim. Trust employees but also use multiple processes to ingrain financial transparency and accountability in all business systems. This reduces opportunity and temptation for theft.

Chapter 10: Investigating Pink-Collar Criminals

Guilt is cancer. Guilt will confine you, torture you, destroy you as an artist. It's a black wall. It's a thief.

—Dave Grohl, American musician

You have this feeling that something just isn't right with your business finances. It might start with some of the pink flags I've described. You may have a nagging suspicion that your accounting numbers don't seem quite right.

For example, let's say that you sold X number of widgets but your bank account doesn't seem to reflect those sales. So you start snooping around. Stop. Please stop! If you walked into your home or office and saw a dead body what would you do? Call 911. You most likely would not touch the crime scene. Yet when a business owner discovers a suspected embezzlement, he or she often starts tampering with the evidence. These are not DIY cases. Why? Because you could end up destroying evidence by accident. You need to call in professionals.

Your first call should be to your attorney. If your attorney isn't experienced in embezzlement or fraud you should ask for a referral. You don't want to have a professional learn about fraud on your time and dollars. The attorney should then retain the services of a fraud examiner or forensic accountant. You also may need to hire a computer forensics expert.

89

If you have an "employee dishonesty" insurance policy, you need to contact your insurance company. There are clauses about the timing of your notification when it comes to the claim. Document everything that you're doing, such as how and when you've contacted your attorney and others.

This leads us to the "now or lifestyle" check to link to the suspected crime. What do I mean by that? I mean paying attention to what your employees are saying and doing. This isn't about stalking them, just that paying attention to your employees' lifestyles may be more valuable than background checks. If you look at the ACFE statistics, most embezzlers don't have criminal histories. Only four percent of the fraudsters in the study had criminal histories.

Anecdotally, every business owner I've interviewed after a theft has taken place tells me stories about how things "just didn't add up" about the suspect. Often, the employees took lots of expensive vacations, spent more money than other staff members and generally lived a lifestyle that was not in sync with their salaries. One example in particular was a dentist client of mine who said, "I should have known when she drove a newer Lexus than I do!" As you probably know, this is what investigators like to call a compelling clue.

Here's another good example of easy-to-spot clues. Larry Keith, the owner and CEO of Entek Manufacturing based in Lebanon, Oregon, asked for an investigation by the Lebanon Police Department after he became suspicious of company accounting irregularities. He noticed a change in executive assistant Rhonda Milligan's behavior and wondered how, on her salary, she could afford assets such as a Cadillac Escalade, a horse arena and several horses.[91]

It turned out that Milligan had embezzled $848,000 over a six-year period. Apparently, she was an authorized personal checking account signatory for James Young, the previous company owner. That was because she was tasked with paying his personal bills. She also stole tens of thousands of dollars from the company's petty cash. Milligan was the assistant to both Young and Keith, but she only stole from Young.

I like to call these two embezzlement discovery examples "parking lot audits." Thank you to Deanne Sullivan, CFE, CPA for that term. Does the car match the salary? Is your $30,000 administrative assistant driving a Tesla, Mercedes or a Range Rover? A desk audit might reveal photos of horses, vacation homes, boats, vacations, etc. that don't seem to align with the employee's pay grade. Those are pink flags to be aware of. That said, remember that this employee's spouse might actually have the income to afford these expensive cars. So don't jump to conclusions too quickly.

Confessions or Denials

Despite what you may think about criminals denying their guilt to their last living breath, embezzlers most often confess to their deeds—unless they're serial embezzlers. Even Rita Crundwell who stole $53.7 million from the Town of Dixon, Illinois "sang like a canary" according to former Mayor Jim Burke.[92] She talked for 90 minutes to the FBI agents, detailing what she had done.

Rita thought she only stolen about $10 million. I call this the two-to-six factor. Whatever amount they say they stole, you might need to multiply it by at least two times and potentially six times. Rita was spot on with her estimate with respect to my multiplication factor, with her being off by $43.7 million just rounding down. So when a bookkeeper takes a check for $1,847, her mind only registers it at $1,000. You can see how the discrepancy can grow over time.

A side note to this confession quirk is how some embezzlers are quite business-like with their crimes and therefore have nicely prepared evidence to hand over to investigators. For example, Burnice Geiger, the embezzler I mentioned previously who stole from her own father's bank, apparently kept excellent records of what she stole.

Also, I have had cases where embezzlers had the Explanation of Benefits receipts—the written evidence— for insurance payments tucked in the back of their desks. I even had a case where an embezzler maintained a detailed spreadsheet for a series of thefts. Nathan Mueller who stole $8.5 million kept immaculate records on his thefts. He even paid taxes on the stolen funds. But Mueller was a CPA and it was in his nature to keep track.

Are these criminals crazy? That may be up for debate but there's an explanation in many cases. Sometimes this behavior can be tied to the criminal's "intent" to eventually pay back the stolen funds.

Paying Back Stolen Funds

How are the embezzlers going to pay back the stolen money? Oddly, most actually do say they planned on paying it back to their employers. If they were gamblers, they'd reimburse the funds when they hit it big one day.

How exactly was this going to happen? Are they going to make a huge account entry and count on no one noticing? One would think that the CPA would question that deposit. That said, I actually have seen some who have paid a little money back over time but they were never even close to the amount stolen when they got caught.

And realistically, if they no longer needed the extra money would they or could they pay it back? Who's going to decide they no longer need the extra money? Hey, life gets more expensive every day and you never know when you'll need an extra few hundred thousand dollars in stolen money!

Get a fraud therapist... Not joking

When you've been a victim of embezzlement you start to question everything and distrust everyone around you. How could I not see this coming? What did I miss? How could I be so stupid?

Second guessing yourself causes all sorts of negative side-effects. You want to take control of everything and trust no one. Work grinds to a halt. Who are you going to talk to? You shouldn't be embarrassed, but you are.

You may not realize it but many people—way more than you know—have been through this same experience. They don't tell family, friends or colleagues either. This is why I'm not kidding when I say you may need a therapist. I don't think your lawyer is going to be your best therapist, especially at $400 plus per hour.

Seeing news stories and people commenting on your—the business owner's—lack of intelligence when it happens doesn't help lift your spirits either. Society rarely comments on someone whose home or business is burglarized even if they left the door unlocked. Yet, people say the meanest things about a business owner who didn't notice all of that missing money as it was being stolen. Victim shaming has no place with respect to any type of crime.

So I say that it might be worth considering some counseling if the experience of an embezzlement is affecting you emotionally. A business owner once told me the hardest part of discovering an embezzlement was telling employees about it. She said, "That was probably one of the most difficult conversations that still tears me up. Those particular employees left their [previous] jobs when we started our company to join us because of the trust and faith they had that we would be successful." Broken trust causes lasting scars.

Chapter 11: Conclusion

Knowing is not enough; We must apply. Willing is not enough; We must do.

—Bruce Lee

I wrote this book because people, especially business owners on Main Street, need to understand how and why embezzlement happens. Speaking and training about pink-collar crime and embezzlement is the most important work I believe I have done in my career. Crime can happen to any business owner. It can happen no matter how smart you are, how much money you've made or where you are on the organization chart.

Mark Cuban was the victim of pink-collar crime after he graduated with his MBA.[93] He thought he had done everything right including writing and signing all of the checks. He gave the written checks to his administrative assistant, Renee, and all she had to do was put them in the envelopes and mail them. What she did was take some white-out and put her name in as the payee. She left him $2,000 out of $84,000. Gosh, that was kind of her. Cuban went on to become a billionaire but he still talks about this story today. He says it was painful but also was the best thing that ever happened to him because it made him get his business management act together.

Embezzlement probably won't be the best thing that happens to you. I will tell you that I had a victim who lost $500,000. It almost ruined that person's business. In the end, things did work out for the better but it was a long, painful process to go through.

Understanding that if you become a victim of embezzlement, it will cause you pain, grief, heartache and questioning of your own beliefs. That's normal. Chances are that wealthy people, astronauts, neurosurgeons and restaurant owners who work every day to build their businesses can and will become victims of a trusted employee gone bad. All you can do is do your best to prevent it or spot it early on.

Unfortunately, fraud happens. But I hope the stories and tips in this book will arm you with the knowledge to decrease your chances of becoming a victim of pink-collar crime and reduce your losses.

APPENDIX & REFERENCES

Appendix: For Victims of Embezzlement

Forgiveness has nothing to do with absolving a criminal of his crime. It has everything to do with relieving oneself of the burden of being a victim—letting go of the pain and transforming oneself from victim to survivor.

—C.R. Strahan

Have you ever wondered if your office manager is stealing from you? If you're reading this chapter, chances are your answer is yes. Unfortunately, embezzlement happens to every type of business. Whether you're a dentist, small business owner, municipal agency, it can happen to anyone.

It didn't happen because you weren't smart. It happened because someone, perhaps your office manager, took advantage of you. That individual saw an opportunity to steal and took it. The fraud triangle has three parts: opportunity, pressure and rationalization. <u>You can only control opportunity.</u>

Respond thoughtfully to suspicions. You need to understand the process of acting on a suspicion of embezzlement. There's no CSI: Embezzlement. These cases take time, patience, understanding and money. Below is a checklist of tasks to be undertaken. Most importantly you need to realize that money is replaceable and time is not. Trust may be difficult to regain within your business. You will look at everyone differently.

Let's get started. Contact the right people first:

1. **The first call is to your attorney.** Don't call just any attorney, but one who specifically handles employment law and fraud. If your regular attorney is not comfortable with this type of case or you are not comfortable with him or her handling it, ask for a referral.

2. **The second call is to your insurance carrier.** If you have employee dishonesty insurance, this is a critical call to make. There are rules about notifying your insurance carrier in a timely manner to retain coverage and file the claim.

3. **Assemble the rest of your fraud team.** This may include a certified fraud examiner, law enforcement, computer forensics specialist and your accountant. One of the most important members of your team may be a therapist. Many victims have told me that they were most affected emotionally by the breach of trust. The long-term, trusted employee whom you had to your home and possibly considered to be part of your family potentially has lied to you for many years. This is devastating.

Other tasks:

- **Computer access:** Remove remote work access (if the employee has it.)

- **Passwords:** Change all passwords ASAP.

- **Physical security:** Change the locks and passcodes ASAP.

- **Credit checks:** Run both personal and business credit checks on your business to identify anomalies.

- **Banking:** Notify your banker(s).

- **Vendors:** Notify your vendors (depending on the position of the employee).

- **Payroll:** Be compliant with state and federal laws when terminating the employee.

- **Staff and clients:** Be careful when notifying staff and clients. You don't want a lawsuit about libeling the employee.

- **Document, document and document.** Consider the suspect's workspace to be a crime scene. Do not disturb it without proper guidance.

And finally, as hard as it is, you need to get back to work. Your job is serving customers, making money, keeping your employees employed, and staying on track. Money is replaceable. Time is not. Stay focused.

If you would like a consultation about suspected embezzlement in your company or organization, please contact me. One-hour consultations are provided for a fixed fee. I encourage you to visit my website at https://kellypaxton.com.

References

[1] Definition of pink-collar crime, *Forbes* magazine, https://www.forbes.com/sites/bruceweinstein/2020/07/08/pink-collar-crime-what-it-is-and-how-to-avoid-becoming-a-target/?sh=5c0374f40f23

[2] *FBI 2019 Semiannual Uniform Crime Report*, https://www.fbi.gov/news/stories/2019-preliminary-semiannual-uniform-crime-report-released-012120

[3] Homicides committed by men, American Psychological Association, https://www.apa.org/monitor/2019/01/ce-corner

[4] *2013 Marquet Report on Embezzlement*, Public Broadcasting, https://mediad.publicbroadcasting.net/p/vpr/files/The_2013_Marquet_Report_On_Embezzlement.pdf

[5] MSNBC "Morning Joe" show at https://www.msnbc.com/morning-joe, https://thehill.com/blogs/blog-briefing-room/news/417102-tom-brokaw-historians-will-say-this-was-the-century-of-women

[6] Bernie Madoff, *Wall Street Journal*, https://www.wsj.com/articles/SB123673521911590783 and Business Insider, https://www.businessinsider.com/how-bernie-madoffs-ponzi-scheme-worked-2014-7

[7] Eleanor Squillari, Bernie Madoff's assistant, *Vanity Fair*, https://www.vanityfair.com/style/2009/05/bernie-madoffs-secretary-spills-his-secrets

[8] Edwin Sutherland, *White Collar Crime*, Yale University Press, 1983, https://www.google.com/books/edition/White_Collar_Crime/U5rYDw AAQBAJ?hl=en&gbpv=1&bsq=may%20be%20defined

[9] Kathleen Daly, PhD, pink-collar crime, Washington & Lee University, https://pinkcrime.academic.wlu.edu/category/the-4-1-1/defining-pink-collar-crime

[10] Rodolfo Olivas, embezzler, *Space Coast Daily*, https://spacecoastdaily.com/2018/04/longtime-bookkeeper-at-west-melbourne-manufacture-company-arrested-for-crimes-totaling-1-3-million

[11] 2016 U.S. Dept. of Labor statistics, https://www.bostonglobe.com/metro/2017/03/06/chart-the-percentage-women-and-men-each-profession/GBX22YsWl0XaeHghwXfE4H/story.html

[12] Crime rates by gender, JRANK, https://law.jrank.org/pages/1250/Gender-Crime-Differences-between-male-female-offending-patterns.html

[13] Freda Alder, *Sisters in Crime: The Rise of the New Female Criminal*, https://web.archive.org/web/20110719194804/http:/www.criminology.fsu.edu/crimtheory/Adler.htm

[14] Gender and crime, JRANK, https://law.jrank.org/pages/1251/Gender-Crime-Explaining-female-offending.html

[15] Cesare Lombroso, Italian physician and criminologist, Wikipedia, https://en.wikipedia.org/wiki/Cesare_Lombroso

[16] Sigmund Freud, *Very Well Mind*, https://www.verywellmind.com/how-sigmund-freud-viewed-women-2795859

[17] Pew Research Foundation, social pressures on women, https://www.pewresearch.org/fact-tank/2018/03/15/for-womens-history-month-a-look-at-gender-gains-and-gaps-in-the-u-s/

[18] Haines, E. L., Deaux, K., & Lofaro, N. (2016), "The times they are a-changing…or are they not? A comparison of gender stereotypes, 1983-2014." *Psychology of Women Quarterly*, 40(3), 353-363. doi:10.1177/0361684316634081

[19] Elizabeth Holmes, founder and former CEO of Theranos, *New York Times*, https://www.nytimes.com/2018/06/15/health/theranos-elizabeth-holmes-fraud.html

[20] Nancy Jackson Carroll, "Millennium Mobster," *Star Telegram*, https://www.star-telegram.com/news/local/community/northeast-tarrant/article192568014.html

[21] Steve Heimoff, Madoff embezzlement victim, National Public Radio, https://www.npr.org/2018/12/23/678238031/for-madoff-victims-scars-remain-10-years-later

[22] Bernie Madoff embezzlement victims, Securities and Exchange Commission, CNBC and *Wall Street Journal*, https://www.sec.gov/litigation/complaints/2009/comp21096.pdf, https://www.cnbc.com/2017/03/28/charles-murphy-investor-burned-by-bernie-madoff-jumps-to-death.html and https://www.wsj.com/articles/SB123439995182175299

[23] White collar crime costs in the U.S., Association of Certified Fraud Examiners, https://www.acfe.com/report-to-the-nations/2020

[24] Crime reporting on business fraud, Federal Bureau of Investigation, https://ucr.fbi.gov/nibrs/nibrs_wcc.pdf

[25] Eugene Soltes, *The Atlantic*, https://www.theatlantic.com/business/archive/2016/12/pyschology-white-collar-criminal/503408

[26] Betrayal by Eugene Block, https://4a7elf2tvomo2jcumx24k867-wpengine.netdna-ssl.com/wp-content/uploads/docs/doc027.pdf

[27] Nora Zelevansky, wife of embezzler, *The Week*, https://theweek.com/articles/463942/husband-embezzled--went-jail

[28] Tina Lemmens and Rick Jacobsen, embezzlement by spouse, *Wall Street Journal*, https://www.wsj.com/articles/so-your-wife-embezzled-500-000-and-the-irs-wants-to-tax-you-1533288602?mod=e2fb

[29] Fraud triangle, *Occupational Fraud and Abuse*, https://books.google.com/books?id=qAQVCgAAQBAJ&pg=PA111&lpg=PA111&dq=joseph+wells+fraud+triangle&source=bl&ots=WsllO3dE9Q&sig=ACfU3U3n9fsBvsjOrNEqCPPqqqw5HRqoVw&hl=en&sa=X&ved=2ahUKEwjImIGzsrrhAhUOuZ4KHWCtB38Q6AEwD3oECAgQAQ#v=onepage&q=joseph%20wells&f=false

[30] Paul Marinaccio, Sr., embezzlement victim, *Buffalo News*, https://buffalonews.com/news/local/crime-and-courts/700-000-embezzlement-from-boss-sends-trusted-cheektowaga-bookkeeper-to-prison/article_c2ada917-c887-5b24-b486-f186f194909a.html

[31] Yvonne Mitchell, embezzler, *Bangor Daily News*, https://bangordailynews.com/2018/01/08/news/bangor/ex-bookkeeper-says-she-stole-from-bangor-area-school-district-to-help-son-on-drugs

[32] Shannon Nagle, embezzler, *Steamboat Pilot and Aspen Daily News*, https://www.steamboatpilot.com/news/aspen-office-manager-steals-660k-from-doctors-office-hides-it-with-fake-quick-books-reports and https://www.aspendailynews.com/news/aspen-woman-who-stole-from-sister-s-medical-practice-nets/article_cfff9c06-7362-11e8-83ac-a33c967772b5.html

[33] Gary Foster, embezzler, *Fraud Conference News*, https://www.fraudconferencenews.com/home/2020/6/24/betrayed-bank-assistant-vice-president-embezzles-22-million-as-payback

[34] Peter C. Orlandi, whistleblower victim, *Courthouse News*, https://www.courthousenews.com/embezzlement-wasnt-his-fault-bank-vp-says

[35] Kimberly Compitello, embezzler, NBC Today Show, https://www.today.com/news/parents-steal-thousands-dollars-school-booster-clubs-2D79736779

[36] Cindy Schorn, embezzler, OregonLive, https://www.oregonlive.com/forest-grove/2014/05/longtime_banks_school_district.html

[37] Volunteerism data from the U.S. Bureau of Labor Statistics, https://www.bls.gov/news.release/volun.t01.htm

[38] Jessica Warner-Reed, embezzler, Channel 3000, https://www.channel3000.com/former-hs-bookkeeper-gets-2-years-prison-for-303k-embezzlement

[39] Most common fraud scheme, Marquet International, https://mediad.publicbroadcasting.net/p/vpr/files/The_2013_Marquet_Report_On_Embezzlement.pdf

[40] Ryan Thorpe, embezzler, *Belleville News-Democrat*, https://www.bnd.com/news/local/article202964984.html

[41] Susan Tranberg, embezzler, OregonLive, https://www.oregonlive.com/crime/2019/10/ex-weyerhaeuser-finance-manager-charged-with-fraud-aggravated-identity-theft.html

[42] Rebecca Jelfo, embezzler, *San Diego Union Tribune*, Patch.com and CBS, https://www.sandiegouniontribune.com/news/sns-bc-md--embezzlement-plea-20190905-story.html, https://patch.com/maryland/silverspring/silver-spring-woman-pleads-guilty-federal-wire-fraud-scheme and https://baltimore.cbslocal.com/2019/12/10/ex-marketing-executive-gets-prison-for-855k-fraud-plot

[43] Amber Crowder and Shauna Brumfield, embezzlers, *Washington Post* and U.S. Department of Justice, https://www.washingtonpost.com/local/public-safety/former-dc-public-schools-employee-and-friend-plead-guilty-to-fraud-in-300000-bid-rigging-scheme/2018/11/26/4a1e25c0-f1bc-11e8-aeea-b85fd44449f5_story.html and https://www.justice.gov/usao-dc/pr/former-dc-schools-employee-and-business-owner-plead-guilty-federal-charge-bid-rigging

[44] Palestine Ace, embezzler, U.S. Department of Justice, https://www.justice.gov/usao-ma/pr/boston-woman-sentenced-27-million-bank-fraud-scheme

[45] Men committing vendor fraud, *2013 Marquet Report on Embezzlement*, https://mediad.publicbroadcasting.net/p/vpr/files/The_2013_Marquet_Report_On_Embezzlement.pdf

[46] Credit card fraud, *2013 Marquet Report on Embezzlement*, https://mediad.publicbroadcasting.net/p/vpr/files/The_2013_Marquet_Report_On_Embezzlement.pdf

[47] Diann Cattani, embezzler, Association of Certified Fraud Examiners , https://www.acfe.com/vid.aspx?id=4294974547

[48] Sean Jelen, embezzler, U.S. Department of Justice, https://www.justice.gov/usao-mdpa/pr/former-ceo-scranton-federal-credit-union-sentenced-70-months-imprisonment

[49] Credit card enabled fraud, APnow, https://www.ap-now.com

[50] Netflix human resources policies, *Harvard Business Review*, https://hbr.org/2014/01/how-netflix-reinvented-hr

[51] Burnice Geiger, embezzler, *New York Times*, https://timesmachine.nytimes.com/timesmachine/1961/02/18/118899642.html?pdf_redirect=true&site=false

[52] Stephen Dubner, *Freakonomics*, https://freakonomics.com

53 Alyssa Costa, embezzler, *Sentinel Colorado*, https://sentinelcolorado.com/orecent-headlines/aurora-woman-sentenced-to-15-years-in-prison-for-stealing-740k-from-paving-company-in-henderson

54 Rita Crundwell, Queen of Pink Collar Crime, *Fraud Magazine*, https://www.fraud-magazine.com/cover-article.aspx?id=4295003585

55 *North & South*, "Why women steal from their employers," https://www.noted.co.nz/currently/currently-crime/the-female-fraud-squad-why-women-steal-from-their-employers

56 *2013 Marquet Report on Embezzlement*, https://mediad.publicbroadcasting.net/p/vpr/files/The_2013_Marquet_Report_On_Embezzlement.pdf

57 Annie Carbullido, *Omaha World-Herald*, https://omaha.com/news/crime/year-old-woman-sentenced-for-embezzling-million-from-employer-using/article_965e1662-3c1d-11e7-aa06-0b6de2539f46.html

58 Nichol Evans, *Lottery Post* and ABC, https://www.lotterypost.com/news/315096 and https://www.abc12.com/content/news/Woman-sentenced-for-embezzling-from-addiction-treatment-center-478694843.html

59 *ACFE 2020 Report to the Nations*, Association of Certified Fraud Examiners, https://www.acfe.com/report-to-the-nations/2020

60 Julie Phillips, *Boston Globe*, https://archive.boston.com/news/local/vermont/articles/2011/10/31/vt_woman_sentenced_to_1_year_prison

61 Paul Klenowski, *Gender, Identity, and Accounts: How White Collar Offenders Do Gender When Making Sense of Their Crimes*, https://www.academia.edu/14923414/Gender_Identity_and_Accounts_

How_White_Collar_Offenders_Do_Gender_When_Making_Sense_of_
Their_Crimes

62 Somerville Homeless Coalition, *Boston Globe*,
https://www3.bostonglobe.com/metro/2018/01/27/taking-from-
charity-employee-theft-shockingly-common-nonprofit-
groups/aGzL6qg5JnhkAsAbj7tMkO/story.html?arc404=true

63 Business losses from fraud, *2018 ACFE's Report to the Nation*,
https://www.acfe.com/report-to-the-nations/2018/Default.aspx

64 Bonnie Brannock Davis, embezzler, *The Roanoke Times*,
https://roanoke.com/news/crime/woman-pleads-guilty-to-embezzling-
from-giles-county-rescue-squad/article_f1d48d45-9ac1-5e73-a2a6-
66117fe6b2d2.html

65 Jerry Hennessey, embezzler, *Duluth News Tribune*,
https://www.duluthnewstribune.com/incoming/6644731-Ashby-
creditors-settle-for-1.5M-from-board-insurance

66 Sister Marie Thornton, embezzler, *New York Post*,
https://nypost.com/2011/11/13/twisted-sister-in-nun-jail

67 *2020 Status of Global Christianity Report*,
https://www.gordonconwell.edu/center-for-global-christianity/wp-
content/uploads/sites/13/2020/01/Status-of-Global-Christianity-
2020.pdf

68 Church fraud, Brotherhood Mutual,
https://www.brotherhoodmutual.com/resources/safety-library/risk-
management-articles/administrative-staff-and-
finance/finances/fraudsters-target-churches

69 *2020 Global Study on Occupational Fraud and Abuse*,
https://www.acfe.com/report-to-the-nations/2020

[70] Minnie Mangum, embezzler, *Pilot Online*
https://www.pilotonline.com/news/article_73d8cafe-ed1e-5102-9004-c0fb1705fdb9.html

[71] Warren Buffett, *Berkshire Hathaway 2018 Annual Letter,*
https://www.berkshirehathaway.com/letters/2018ltr.pdf

[72] Susan Fowler, Uber engineer, Susan J. Fowler blog,
https://www.susanjfowler.com/blog/2017/2/19/reflecting-on-one-very-strange-year-at-uber

[73] *Report to the Nations' 2020 Global Study on Occupational Fraud and Abuse,*
https://www.bswllc.com/assets/htmldocuments/2020-Report-to-the-Nations.pdf

[74] *ACFE 2018 Report to the Nations,* Punishment for fraud,
https://www.acfe.com/report-to-the-nations/2018/Default.aspx

[75] Medical clinic embezzlement, Washington County, Oregon,
https://www.co.washington.or.us/Sheriff/News/sheriffs-office-news.cfm?issue=Mar_2009

[76] Employee theft, Better Business Bureau,
https://www.orsurety.com/blog/30-percent-of-business-failures-are-caused-by-employee-theft

[77] Roseann Robyn Kipp, *The Missoulian,*
https://missoulian.com/news/local/eureka-woman-sentenced-for-embezzlement-that-closed-eureka-economic-development/article_8c0eb7f6-b0b5-56df-a343-ef404f1e5314.html

[78] Gary Foster, embezzler, *Fraud Conference News,*
https://www.fraudconferencenews.com/home/2020/6/24/betrayed-bank-assistant-vice-president-embezzles-22-million-as-payback

[79] Medical practice theft, LSL CPAs and Advisors,
https://lslcpas.com/medical-office-embezzlement-are-you-at-risk

[80] Dental practice theft, ADA Center for Professional Success, https://success.ada.org/en/practice-management/finances/ada-survey-employee-theft-in-the-dental-practice?utm_medium=VanityUrl

[81] Prosperident's Hall of Shame, https://www.prosperident.com/prosperidents-hall-shame-gallery

[82] Elizabeth Eisert, embezzler, Prosperident, https://www.prosperident.com/elizabeth-ann-eisert-connvicted-embezzling-450k-dentist-sentenced-60-months

[83] Kristina Vargas, embezzler, *Citizens Journal,* https://www.citizensjournal.us/dental-office-worker-arrested-for-allegedly-obtaining-fraudulent-prescriptions

[84] Lisa Marie Sundquist, embezzler, OregonLive, https://www.oregonlive.com/portland/2012/02/southwest_portland_office_mana.html

[85] Linda Renae Williams, embezzler, *The Gainesville Sun,* https://www.gainesville.com/news/20200219/gpd-woman-tried-to-kill-boss-ndash-twice-ndash-to-hide-fraud-scheme

[86] Lori Isenberg, embezzler, *Washington Post,* https://www.washingtonpost.com/nation/2020/02/28/murder-drowning-lake-benadryl

[87] Certified Fraud Examiner Code of Ethics, Association of Certified Fraud Examiners, https://www.acfeinsights.com/acfe-insights/acfe-code-of-professional-ethics#:~:text=ACFE%20members%20are%20not%20allowed,all%20the%20rule%20is%20saying

[88] Walt Pavlo, "White Collar Wives," *Forbes,* https://www.forbes.com/sites/walterpavlo/2019/02/25/ten-things-every-spouse-of-a-white-collar-defendant-should-know/#1b821552f211

[89] Neutralization, Wikipedia,
https://en.wikipedia.org/wiki/Techniques_of_neutralization

[90] "Gender, Identity, and Accounts: How White Collar Offenders Do Gender When Making Sense of Their Crimes" by Paul M. Klenowski, Heith Copes and Christopher W. Mullin, *Justice Quarterly*, https://www.tandfonline.com/doi/abs/10.1080/07418825.2010.482536

[91] Rhonda Milligan, embezzler, *Lebanon Express*, https://lebanon-express.com/news/local/milligan-pleads-guilty-to-embezzlement/article_42504304-a9df-11e1-9a1d-0019bb2963f4.html

[92] Rita Crundwell, embezzler, U.S. Department of Justice, https://www.justice.gov/usao-ndil/pr/former-dixon-comptroller-rita-crundwell-sentenced-nearly-20-years-federal-prison-537

[93] Mark Cuban, CNBC, https://www.cnbc.com/2020/02/06/mark-cuban-had-82000-dollars-stolen-from-his-first-company.html